W9-BLN-843

BREAKFAST WITH THE POPE

120 DAILY READINGS

Pope John Paul II

*Selected by the editors of
Servant Publications*

GRAMERCY BOOKS
NEW YORK

Scripture texts used in this work are usually taken from the New American Bible, copyright © 1970 by the Confraternity of Christian Doctrine, Washington, D.C. All rights reserved. Selected texts are from the Revised Standard Version of the Bible (RSV), © 1946, 1952, 1971 by the Division of Christian Education of the National Council of the Churches of Christ in the USA. All rights reserved.

Servant Publications wishes to thank Edizioni Piemme, S.P.A. (Via del Carmine 5, 15033 Casale Monferrato, Italy) for permission to reprint excerpts from *Message of Love*, © 1986 in this work.

Interior photos: Bettmann. Used by permission

This 2003 edition is published by Gramercy Books, an imprint of Random House Value Publishing, a division of Random House, Inc., New York, by arrangement with Servant Publications.

Gramercy is a registered trademark and the colophon is a trademark of Random House, Inc.

Random House
New York • Toronto • London • Sydney • Auckland
www.randomhouse.com

Printed and bound in Singapore.

A catalog record for this title is available from the Library of Congress.

ISBN 0-517-22254-X

10 9 8 7 6 5 4 3 2 1

Let yourselves be charmed by Christ, the Infinite who appeared among you in visible and imitable form. Let yourselves be attracted by his example, which has changed the history of the world and directed it toward an exhilarating goal. Let yourselves be loved by the love of the Holy Spirit, who wishes to turn you away from worldly things to begin in you the life of the new self, created in God's way in righteousness and true holiness.

Fall in love with Jesus Christ, to live his very life, so that our world may have life in the light of the gospel.

ABBREVIATIONS

AAS	*Acta Apostolicae Sedis*
CCL	*Corpus Christianorum, Series Latina*
CSEL	*Corpus Scriptorum Ecclesiasticorum Latinorum*
FF	*Fonti Francescane* (Franciscan Sources)
LG	Second Ecumenical Vatican Council, Dogmatic Constitution on the Church *(Lumen Gentium)*
SC	Second Ecumenical Vatican Council, Constitution on the Sacred Liturgy *(Sacrosanctum Concilium)*
PG	J.P. Migne, ed., *Patrologia Graeca*
TPS	*The Pope Speaks* (published bimonthly by *Our Sunday Visitor* (Huntington, IN; 1-800-248-3440)

Do Not Be Afraid

To all people of today, I once again repeat the impassioned cry with which I began my pastoral ministry: "Do not be afraid! Open, indeed, open wide the doors to Christ!" Open to his saving power the confines of states, and systems political and economic, as well as the vast fields of culture, civilization, and development. Do not be afraid. Christ knows 'what is inside a person.' Only he knows! Today too often people do not know what they carry inside, in the deepest recesses of their soul, in their heart. Too often people are uncertain about a sense of life on earth. Invaded by doubts they are led into despair. Therefore—with humility and trust I beg and implore you—allow Christ to speak to the person in you. Only he has the words of life, yes, eternal life.

Beyond Ourselves

At the climax of revelation, the incarnate Word proclaims, "I am the life" (Jn 14:6), and "I came that they might have life" (Jn 10:10). But what life? Jesus' intention was clear: the very life of God, which surpasses all the possible aspirations of the human heart (see 1 Cor 2:9). The fact is that through the grace of baptism we are already God's children (see 1 Jn 3:1-2).

Jesus came to meet men and women, to heal the sick and the suffering, to free those possessed by devils and to raise the dead. He gave himself on the cross and rose again from the dead, revealing that he is the Lord of life—the author and the source of life without end.

Our daily experience tells us that life is marked by sin and threatened by death, despite the desire for good which beats in our hearts and the desire for life that courses through our veins. However little heed we pay to the frustrations which life brings us, we discover that everything within us urges us to transcend ourselves, to overcome the temptation of superficiality or despair. It is then that human beings are called to become disciples of that other One who infinitely transcends them, in order to enter at last into true life.

Finding New Life

Left to ourselves, we could never achieve the ends for which we have been created. Within us there is a promise which we find we are incapable of attaining. But the Son of God who came among us has given us his personal assurance: "I am the way, and the truth, and the life" (Jn 14:6). As St. Augustine so strikingly phrased it, Christ "wishes to create a place in which it is possible for all people to find true life." This "place" is his body and his Spirit, in which the whole of human life, redeemed and forgiven, is renewed and made divine....

In the mystery of his cross and resurrection, Christ has destroyed death and sin. He has bridged the infinite distance that separates all people from new life in him. "I am the resurrection and the life," he proclaims. "Whoever believes in me, though he should die, will come to life, and whoever is alive and believes in me will never die" (Jn 11:25).

Christ achieves all this by pouring out his Spirit, the giver of life, in the sacraments; especially in baptism, the sacrament by which the fragile life which we receive from our parents and which is destined to end in death becomes instead a path to eternity; in the sacrament of penance which continually renews God's life within us by the forgiveness of sins; and in the Eucharist, the "bread of life" (see Jn 6:34), which feeds the "living" and gives strength to their steps during their pilgrimage on earth.

❧4❧

On the Emmaus Road with Jesus

"With that their eyes were opened and they recognized him, but he vanished from their sight. Then they said to each other, 'Were not our hearts burning inside us as he talked to us on the road and explained the Scriptures to us?'" (Lk 24:31-32). We who belong to the present generation of those who confess Christ must seek to have the same experience as the two disciples on the road to Emmaus. Let us pray, "Lord Jesus, make us understand the Scriptures; let our hearts burn inside us as you talk to us."

Let our hearts burn! Faith cannot be only cold, hard facts calculated and weighed by our intellect. No, faith must be quickened by love. It must come alive through the good works which reveal God's truth in us.

So we, too, inherit from the apostles the witness they gave, even if we are not direct eyewitnesses of the resurrection. We become witnesses to Christ ourselves. Being a Christian must mean being a witness for Christ.

Love without Limits

Jesus brings God's commandments to fulfillment, particularly the commandment of love of neighbor, by interiorizing their demands and by bringing out their fullest meaning. Love of neighbor springs from a loving heart. Precisely because it loves, it is ready to live out the loftiest challenges. Jesus shows that the commandments must not be understood as a minimum limit not to be gone beyond, but rather as a path involving a moral and spiritual journey toward perfection, at the heart of which is love (see Col 3:14).

Thus the commandment "you shall not murder" becomes a call to an attentive love which protects and promotes the life of one's neighbor. The precept prohibiting adultery becomes an invitation to a pure way of looking at others, capable of respecting the spousal meaning of the body.... Jesus himself is the living "fulfillment" of the law inasmuch as he fulfills its authentic meaning by the total gift of himself: He himself becomes a living and personal law, who invites people to follow him. Through the Spirit, he gives the grace to share his own life and love and provides the strength to bear witness to that love in personal choices and actions (see Jn 13:34-35).

❧6❧

Merciful Justice

God, who is always merciful even when he punishes, "put a mark on Cain, lest anyone should kill him at sight" (Gn 4:15). He thus gave him a distinctive sign, not to condemn him to the hatred of others, but to protect and defend him from those wishing to kill him, even out of a desire to avenge Abel's death. Not even a murderer loses his personal dignity, and God himself pledges to guarantee this. And it is precisely here that the paradoxical mystery of the merciful justice of God is shown forth.

As St. Ambrose writes: "God drove Cain out of his presence and sent him into exile far away from his native land, so that he passed from a life of human kindness to one which was more akin to the rude existence of a wild beast. God, who preferred the correction rather than the death of a sinner, did not desire that a homicide be punished by the exaction of another act of homicide."[1]

Make Peace Your Aim

To reverse the current trend in the arms race involves a parallel struggle on two fronts: on the one side, an immediate and urgent struggle by governments to reduce progressively and equally their armaments; on the other hand, a more patient but nonetheless necessary struggle at the level of the consciences of peoples to take their responsibility in regard to the ethical cause of the insecurity that breeds violence. They must come to grips with the material and spiritual inequalities of our world....

Peace... must become the goal of all men and women of good will. Unhappily still in our days, sad realities cast their shadows across the international horizon. They cause the suffering of destruction, such that they could cause humanity to lose the hope of being able to master its own future... in the collaboration of peoples.

Despite the suffering that invades my soul, I feel empowered, even obliged, solemnly to reaffirm before all the world what my predecessors and I myself have repeated so often in the name of conscience, in the name of morality, in the name of humanity, and in the name of God:

Peace is not a utopia, nor an inaccessible ideal, nor an unrealizable dream.

War is not an inevitable calamity.

Peace is possible.

And because it is possible, peace is our duty: our grave duty, our supreme responsibility.

❧8❧

If You Want Peace, Serve the Poor

The divine master has taught us by his words the demanding features of that poverty which leads us to true freedom. He who "though he was in the form of God, did not deem equality with God something to be grasped at. Rather, he emptied himself and took the form of a slave" (Phil 2:6-7). He was born in poverty. He lived as one who had "nowhere to lay his head" (Mt 8:20). He... suffered the death reserved for criminals. He called the poor blessed and assured them that the kingdom of God belonged to them (see Lk 6:20). He reminded the rich that it is difficult for them to enter the kingdom of God (see Mk 10:25).

Christ's example, no less than his words, is normative for Christians. We know that at the last judgment we shall all be judged without distinction on our practical love of our brothers and sisters. On that day it will be in the practical love they have shown that many will discover that they have in fact met Christ, although without having known him before in an explicit way (see Mt 25:35-37).

"If you want peace, reach out to the poor!" May rich and poor recognize that they are brothers and sisters. May they share what they have with one another as children of the one God who loves everyone, who wills the good of everyone, and who offers to everyone the gift of peace!

On Pilgrimage to the Light that Never Sets

The Second Vatican Council speaks of the pilgrim church, establishing an analogy with the Israel of the Old Covenant journeying through the desert. The journey also has an external character, visible in the time and space in which it historically takes place. For the church "is destined to extend to all regions of the earth and so to enter into the history of mankind," but at the same time "she transcends all limits of time and space."[2]

And yet the essential character of her pilgrimage is interior: it is a question of a pilgrimage through faith, by "the power of the Risen Lord,"[3] a pilgrimage in the Holy Spirit, given to the church as the invisible Comforter... (see Jn 14:26; 15:26; 16:7). [As the council said,] "Moving forward through trial and tribulation, the church is strengthened by the power of God's grace promised to her by the Lord, so that... moved by the Holy Spirit, she may never cease to renew herself, until through the cross she arrives at the light which knows no setting."[4]

We Are All "Elder Sons"

The parable of the prodigal son is above all the story of the inexpressible love of a Father—God—who offers to his son, when he comes back to him, the gift of full reconciliation. But when the parable evokes, in the figure of the elder son, the selfishness which divides the brothers, it also becomes the story of the human family: It describes our situation and shows the path to be followed.

The prodigal son... represents those who are aware of the existence in their inmost hearts of a longing for reconciliation at all levels and without reserve. They realize with an inner certainty that this reconciliation is possible only if it derives from a first and fundamental reconciliation—the one which brings a person back from distant separation to filial friendship with God, whose infinite mercy is clearly known.

But if the parable is read from the point of view of the other son, it portrays the situation of the human family, divided by forms of selfishness. It throws light on the difficulty involved in satisfying the desire and longing for one reconciled and united family. It therefore reminds us of the need for a profound transformation of hearts through the rediscovery of the father's mercy and through victory over misunderstanding and over hostility among brothers and sisters.

The Gift of Reconciliation

The story of the Garden of Eden makes us think about the tragic consequences of rejecting the Father, which becomes evident in humanity's inner disorder and in the breakdown of harmony between man and woman, brother and brother. Also significant is the gospel parable of the two brothers who, in different ways, distance themselves from their father and cause a rift between them. Refusal of God's fatherly love and of his loving gifts is always at the root of humanity's divisions.

But we know that God, "rich in mercy" (see Eph 2:4), like the father in the parable, does not close his heart to any of his children. He waits for them, looks for them, goes to meet them at the place where the refusal of communion imprisons them in isolation and division. He calls them to gather about his table in the joy of the feast of forgiveness and reconciliation.

This initiative on God's part is made concrete and manifest in the redemptive act of Christ, which radiates through the world by means of the ministry of the church.

❧12❧

Your Holy Family

"At the beginning of the New Testament, as at the beginning of the Old, there is a married couple. But whereas Adam and Eve were the source of evil which was unleashed on the world, Joseph and Mary are the summit from which holiness spreads all over the earth. The Savior began the work of salvation by this virginal and holy union, wherein is manifested his all-powerful will to purify and sanctify the family—that sanctuary of love and cradle of life."[5] How much the family of today can learn from [these words of Pope Paul VI]!

"The essence and role of the family are in the final analysis specified by love. Hence the family has the mission to guard, reveal and communicate love, and this is a living reflection of and a real sharing in God's love for humanity and the love of Christ the Lord for the church his bride."[6] So, it is in the Holy Family, the original "church in miniature,"[7]...that every Christian family must be reflected.

❦13❦

Discovering Your True Self in Christ

Man cannot live without love. He remains a being that is incomprehensible to himself. His life is senseless if love is not revealed to him—if he does not encounter love, if he does not experience it and make it his own, if he does not participate intimately in it. This... is why Christ the Redeemer fully reveals man to himself....

The man who wishes to understand himself thoroughly... must with his unrest, uncertainty and even his weakness and sinfulness, with his life and death, draw near to Christ. He must enter Christ with all his own self. He must appropriate and assimilate the whole of the reality of the incarnation and redemption in order to find himself. If this profound process takes place within him, he then bears fruit not only of adoration of God but also of deeper wonder at himself.

❧14❧

Intimacy with God

As he parted with the apostles on the eve of his Passion, Jesus said: "Anyone who loves me will be true to my word, and my Father will love him; and we will come to him and make our dwelling place with him" (Jn 14:23). Just a few moments before being handed over to death, he reveals the heights and depths of an immense love. He reveals to us the mystery of God's indwelling presence. Yes, man is called to become a temple for the Blessed Trinity. What greater degree of communion with God could man ever aspire to?

What greater proof than this could God ever give us of his saving love? The God of all wants to enter into communion with man. All the age-old history of Christian mysticism, even with some of its most sublime expressions, can speak only imperfectly to us about the unutterable presence of God in our hearts.

❧15❧

Our Passion for Prayer

"Lord, teach us to pray" (Lk 11:1). When on the slopes of the Mount of Olives, the apostles addressed Jesus with these words, they were not asking an ordinary question. With spontaneous trust, they were expressing one of the deepest needs of the human heart.

To tell the truth, today's world does not make much room for that need. The hectic pace of daily activity, combined with the noisy and often frivolous invasiveness of the means of communication, is certainly not something conducive to the interior recollection required for prayer....

Because they are creatures and of themselves incomplete and needy, human beings spontaneously turn to him who is the source of every gift, in order to praise him and make intercession. In him they seek to fulfill the tormenting desire which enflames their hearts. St. Augustine understood this quite well when he noted: "You have made us for yourself, O Lord, and our hearts are restless until they rest in you."[8]

Spirit-Led Prayer

Wherever people are praying in the world, there the Holy Spirit is, the living breath of prayer.... Prayer is also the revelation of that abyss which is the heart of man: a depth which comes from God and which only God can fill, precisely with the Holy Spirit. We read in Luke: "If you, with all your sins, know how to give your children good things, how much more will the heavenly Father give the Holy Spirit to those who ask him" (Lk 11:13).

The Holy Spirit is the gift that comes into man's heart together with prayer. In prayer he manifests himself first of all and above all as the gift that "helps us in our weakness." This is the magnificent thought developed by St. Paul in the Letter to the Romans, when he writes: "For we do not know how to pray as we ought; but the Spirit himself makes intercession for us with groanings which cannot be expressed in speech" (Rom 8:26).

Therefore, the Holy Spirit not only enables us to pray, but guides us "from within" in prayer: he is present in our prayer and gives it a divine dimension. Thus "He who searches hearts knows what the Spirit means, for the Spirit intercedes for the saints as God himself wills" (Rom 8:27). Prayer through the power of the Holy Spirit becomes the ever more mature expression of the new man, who by means of this prayer participates in the divine life.

❧17❧

The Attraction of Holiness

The new evangelization will show its authenticity and unleash all its missionary force when it is carried out through the gift not only of the word proclaimed but also of the word lived. In particular, the life of holiness which is resplendent in so many members of the people of God, humble and often unseen, constitutes the simplest and most attractive way to perceive at once the beauty of truth, the liberating force of God's love, and the value of unconditional fidelity to all the demands of the Lord's law, even in the most difficult situations.

For this reason, the church, as a wise teacher of morality, has always invited believers to seek and to find in the saints, and above all in the virgin mother of God "full of grace" and "all-holy," the model, the strength and the joy needed to live a life in accordance with God's commandments and the beatitudes of the gospel.

❧18❧

The Mother of Christians

The Second Vatican Council proclaims: "...the Mother of God is a type of the church in the matter of faith, charity and perfect union with Christ...."⁹

The Council sees the church's motherhood, which is modeled on Mary's, in the fact that the church "brings forth to a new and immortal life children who are conceived of the Holy Spirit and born of God." Here we find echoed St. Paul's words about "the children with whom I am again in travail" (see Gal 4:19), in the same way as a mother gives birth. When, in the Letter to the Ephesians, we read about Christ as the spouse who "nourishes and cherishes" the church as his body (see 5:29), we cannot fail to link this spousal solicitude on the part of Christ above all with the gift of Eucharistic food, similar to the many maternal concerns associated with "nourishing and cherishing" a child.

Joseph's Total Surrender

The same aura of silence that envelops everything else about Joseph also shrouds his work as a carpenter in the house of Nazareth. It is, however, a silence that reveals in a special way the inner portrait of the man. The gospels speak exclusively of what Joseph "did." Still, they allow us to discover in his "actions"—shrouded in silence as they are—an aura of deep contemplation. Joseph was in daily contact with the mystery "hidden from ages past," and which "dwelt" under his roof....

The total sacrifice, whereby Joseph surrendered his whole existence to the demands of the Messiah's coming into his home, becomes understandable only in the light of his profound interior life. It was from this interior life, [said Pope Paul VI,] that "very singular commands and consolations came. They brought him also the logic and strength that belong to simple and clear souls. They gave him the power of making great decisions—such as the decision to... accept the conditions, the responsibility and the burden of a family; but, through an incomparable virginal love, to renounce that natural conjugal love that is the foundation and nourishment of the family."[10]

Listening for God's Call

God calls me and sends me forth as a laborer in his vineyard. He calls me and sends me forth to work for the coming of his kingdom in history....

From eternity God has thought of us and has loved us as unique individuals. Every one of us he called by name, as the Good Shepherd "calls his sheep by name" (see Jn 10:3). However, only in the unfolding of our lives in the events of history is the eternal plan of God revealed to each of us. Therefore, it is a gradual process; in a certain sense, one that happens day by day.

To be able to discover the actual will of the Lord in our lives always involves the following: a receptive listening to the word of God and the church, fervent and constant prayer, recourse to a wise and loving spiritual guide, and a faithful discernment of the gifts and talents given by God, as well as the diverse social and historic situations in which one lives.... No one must forget that the Lord, as the master of the laborers in the vineyard, calls at every hour of life so as to make his holy will more precisely and explicitly known. Therefore, the fundamental and continuous attitude of the disciple should be one of vigilance and a conscious attentiveness to the voice of God.

❦21❦

The Seed of Joy in Suffering

In the perspective of redemption, Christ's passion is oriented toward the resurrection. Human beings too are thus associated with the mystery of the cross in order to share joyfully in the mystery of the resurrection.

For this reason Jesus did not hesitate to proclaim the blessedness of those who suffer: "Blest too are the sorrowing; they shall be consoled" (Mt. 5:4).... This blessedness can only be understood if one admits that human life is not limited to the time spent on earth, but is wholly directed to perfect joy and fullness of joy in the hereafter.

Earthly suffering, when accepted in love, is like a bitter kernel containing the seed of new life, the treasure of divine glory to be given man in eternity. Although the sight of a world burdened with evil and misfortunes of every sort is often so wretched, nevertheless the hope of a better world of love and grace is hidden within it. It is hope that is nourished on Christ's promise. With this support, those who suffer united with him already experience in this life a joy that can seem humanly unexplainable. Heaven in fact begins on earth, beatitude is anticipated in the beatitudes. "In holy people," St. Thomas Aquinas said, "there is a beginning of future happiness."[11]

Surrender Your Suffering to God

We are called to entrust our lives completely to our providential God. As the psalmist tell us: "I have stilled and quieted my soul like a weaned child. Like a weaned child on its mother's lap, [so is my soul within me]" (Ps 131:2). Yet we are afraid to abandon ourselves to God as our Lord and Savior at times. Our mind may be darkened by problems. We forget about our Creator. Or we are really suffering and we doubt God's love for us as our Father.

Yet God's heart of providence is very close to us when we suffer. There are many examples in Scripture. For instance, Job does not hesitate to cry out to God, even in the midst of his suffering. Job shows amazing confidence in God. This confidence is not unfounded. The word of God does indicate that the providence of God, his saving power, is poured out on his people in their hour of greatest need, for they are his children. Job, sick in his body and in his heart, exclaims: "Oh, that today I might find him, that I might come to his judgment seat! I would set out my cause before him, and fill my mouth with arguments" (Jb 23:3-4). Let us come today before our Father with our needs!

❧23❧

St. Claude La Colomobiere's Heart for Christ

In the middle of the seventeenth century, Claude La Colombiere entered the Society of Jesus at a young age. He exercised his mission in Paris and in several provinces. He had a notable influence because of his intellectual effort and because of the dynamism of the Christian life which he knew how to communicate....

Fr. Claude forged his spirituality in the school of the *[Spiritual] Exercises*. He dedicated himself to meditating a great deal on the life of Jesus Christ who is a model for our own life. Contemplating Christ allowed him to live in familiarity with him. "I see" he said, "that I absolutely must belong to him totally...."[12]

This pure-hearted and free religious was prepared to understand and to preach the message that the Heart of Jesus was entrusting to Sr. Margaret Mary Alacoque at the same time.... He received from her the message which would have great repercussions: "Behold the Heart which has so loved men that it spared nothing to exhaust and consume itself in testimony of its love."[13] The Lord asked that a feast be established to honor his heart.... Margaret Mary passed on... to Fr. La Colombiere the mission of establishing this devotion....

Fr. Claude gave himself completely to the Sacred Heart "ever burning with love." Even in trials he practiced forgetfulness of self in order to attain purity of love and to raise the world to God.

Music and Human Harmony

Music has a universal language.... I also think of the significant and unique associating value that music develops. Just as harmony is created in the assonance of notes, so the practice of music in a group produces solidarity, unity of hearts, and friendship. It would not be possible to practice music without allowing yourself to become involved in a common movement, in a conscious tuning of intentions, in an agreement of sounds and of actions. In this sense, art can be considered an invitation to participate in a common and noble work, which elevates and strengthens sentiment.

Such a way of thinking appears even more valid when music gives joy to feasts and celebrations of the community. In that way, people experience feelings of joy and of prayer, of enthusiasm, and of deep action—as music succeeds in inspiring service to God and others.

Music as art is therefore an appeal to meditate on beauty, which springs from God, and an invitation to consider the harmony of creation. Thus, may all of us know how to praise God using music, following the wonderfully harmonized words of Haydn in the famous oratorio *The Creation:* "Choirs of men, choirs of the worlds, voices, orchestras, may all resound: Praised be God for eternity!"

❧25❧

Art and the Human Spirit

Artists are counted among the greatest benefactors of mankind. They are some of the most effective workers for mankind's salvation, since they nourish a person's sense of spirituality. When man contemplates art and its beauty, he abandons himself to it as a source of inspiration. His spiritual sense is heightened. He feels and senses the fascination of pure spirituality. He glimpses God, who is the origin and goal of all created spirituality.

Deeply aware of all this, [said the Second Vatican Council,] the church "has always favored liberal arts, and has always sought their noble service.... She has allowed the artistic forms of every age. Thus, she has formed, through the course of the centuries, an artistic treasure that is to be preserved with the greatest care."[14]

The arts of our time—of all peoples and nations—find freedom of expression in the church, as long as they serve God with due reverence and honor.

26

Women: First and Equal

Women are the first at the tomb. They are the first to find it empty. They are the first to hear "He is not here. He has been raised, exactly as he promised"(Mt 28:6). They are the first to embrace his feet (see Mt 28:9). They are also the first to be called to announce this truth to the apostles (see Mt 28:1-10; Lk 24:8-11).

The Gospel of John emphasizes the special role of Mary Magdalene.... She was the first eyewitness to the risen Christ. For this reason she was also the first to bear witness to him before the apostles. This event, in a sense, crowns all that has been said about Christ entrusting divine truths to women as well as men.... One can say that this fulfilled the words of the prophet: "I will pour out my spirit upon all mankind. Your sons and your daughters shall prophesy" (Joel 3:1).

To "prophesy" means to express by one's words and one's life "the mighty works of God" (see Acts 2:11), preserving the truth and originality of each person, whether woman or man. Gospel "equality," the "equality" of women and men in regard to the "mighty works of God"... constitutes the most obvious basis for the dignity and vocation of women in the church and in the world.

The Secret of Femininity

The Marian dimension of Christian life takes on special importance in relation to women and their status. In fact, femininity has a unique relationship with the mother of the Redeemer.... The figure of Mary of Nazareth sheds light on womanhood as such by the very fact that God, in the sublime event of the incarnation of his Son, entrusted himself to the ministry, the free and active ministry of a woman. It can thus be said that women, by looking to Mary, find in her the secret of living their femininity with dignity and of achieving their own true advancement. In the light of Mary, the church sees in the face of women the reflection of a beauty which mirrors the loftiest sentiments of which the human heart is capable: the self-offering totality of love; the strength that is capable of bearing the greatest sorrows; limitless fidelity and tireless devotion to work; the ability to combine penetrating intuition with words of support and encouragement.

28

Immersed in the Death and Life of Christ

Through the rite of baptism—which is the first of the sacraments of salvation instituted by Jesus—the human person is incorporated into Christ and united to the family of the living God. St. Paul repeats for us what he wrote to the Christians of Rome in his own time: "Are you not aware that we who were baptized into Christ Jesus were baptized into his death? Through baptism into his death we were buried with him, so that, just as Christ was raised from the dead by the glory of the Father, we too might live a new life. If we have been united with him through likeness to his death, so shall we be through a like resurrection" (Rom 6:3-5).

The Apostle Paul teaches us that baptism is a figure and expression of the passion of Christ. In fact, in baptism we are immersed in Christ's death, cleansed of the filth of sin, introduced to the new life of the resurrection, and made living temples of the Spirit. Through baptism we are incorporated into the life of the church. This is the community of Christ the Lord, created and nourished by love. This is the community of faith and new life, which accompanies us in life and sustains us in our weaknesses. Then we are no longer slaves of the greatest evil of all, which is sin. We may begin to live in the fullness of freedom as the children of God.

We Have Become Christ

Following Christ is not an outward imitation, since it touches man at the very depths of his being. Being a follower of Christ means becoming conformed to him who became a servant even to giving himself on the cross (see Phil 2:5-8). Christ dwells by faith in the heart of the believer (see Eph 3:17), and thus the disciple is conformed to the Lord. This is the effect of grace, of the active presence of the Holy Spirit in us.

Having become one with Christ, the Christian becomes a member of his body, which is the church (see 1 Cor 12:13, 27). By the work of the Spirit, baptism radically configures the faithful to Christ in the paschal mystery of death and resurrection; it "clothes him" in Christ (see Gal 3:27): "Let us rejoice and give thanks," exclaims St. Augustine speaking to the baptized, "for we have become not only Christians, but Christ.... Marvel and rejoice: We have become Christ!"[15]

❧30❧

The Prototype of All Christian Families

Through God's mysterious design, it was in the Holy Family of Nazareth that the Son of God spent long years of a hidden life. It is therefore the prototype and example for all Christian families. It was unique in the world. Its life was passed in anonymity and silence in a little town in Palestine. It underwent trials of poverty, persecution, and exile. It glorified God in an incomparably exalted and pure way. And it will not fail to help Christian families—indeed all the families in the world—to be faithful to their day-to-day duties, to bear the cares and tribulations of life, to be open and generous to the needs of others, and to fulfill with joy the plan of God in their regard.

St. Joseph was "a just man," a tireless worker, the upright guardian of those entrusted to his care. May he always guard, protect, and enlighten families.

May the Virgin Mary, who is the mother of the church, also be the mother of "the church of the home." Thanks to her motherly aid, may each Christian family really become a "little church...."

May Christ the Lord, the universal king, the king of families, be present in every Christian home as he was at Cana, bestowing light, joy, serenity and strength.... I beg of him that every family may generously make its own contribution to the coming of his kingdom in the world....

❦31❦

The Family,
School for Evangelizers

In our time, a time of new evangelization, it is urgent for Christian parents to take special care in educating their children to be courageous witnesses of the Savior in today's world. By becoming the first catechists of their own children, they themselves can more easily instill in them a unique love for God's word. By conforming their lives to the gospel each day, parents encourage children in the consistent and generous choices that belong to every true disciple of the Lord.

Let us pray that every Christian family may be a little missionary church and a school for evangelizers. Let us entrust this mission of all believing families, together with their joys and sufferings, to the Immaculate Virgin.... May Mary be their example and their guide, especially an example and guide for families!

❧32❧

The Miracle of Mercy

Christ came not to condemn but to forgive, to show mercy (see Mt 9:13). And the greatest mercy of all is found in his being in our midst and calling us to meet him and to confess, with Peter, that he is "the Son of the living God" (Mt 16:16). No human sin can erase the mercy of God or prevent him from unleashing all his triumphant power, if we only call upon him. Indeed, sin itself makes even more radiant the love of the Father. In order to ransom a slave, he sacrificed his Son: his mercy toward us is redemption.

This mercy reaches its fullness in the gift of the Spirit, who bestows new life and demands that it be lived. No matter how many and great the obstacles put in his way by human frailty and sin, the Spirit, who renews the face of the earth (see Ps 104:30), makes possible the miracle of the perfect accomplishment of the good. This renewal gives the ability to do what is good, noble, beautiful, pleasing to God and in conformity with his will. It is in some way the flowering of the gift of mercy, which offers liberation from the slavery of evil and gives the strength to sin no more. Through the gift of new life, Jesus makes us sharers in his love and leads us to the Father in the Spirit.

A Radical Strike Against Sin

We must be radical with sin. If we do not strike with the ax at the root of selfishness, it will surface again and again. We cannot make progress in the ways of God without making this decision.

The way has been so dramatically laid out for us in Jesus' temptations in the desert. We see him reject the deception of selfish ambition and pride to fully obey his divine call. By renouncing all ambition, he perfectly fulfilled the word of God and submitted to the Father's will.

Obeying Scripture as the Word of God, Jesus overcame the temptation of independence from God when he told the tempter, "Not on bread alone shall man live" (Lk 4:4). He rejected the temptation to work wonders on his own when Satan insinuated, "If you are the Son of God, throw yourself down from here" (Lk 4:9). He also rejected vain ambition and lust for power when the tempter offered him earthly kingdoms. "I will give you all this power," the Evil One told the Christ (Lk 4:6). By overcoming these three temptations, which the people of Israel had fallen into while wandering in the desert, Jesus gave us an example of how we are to act when confronted by deceptions.

❧34❧

Repairing Sin's Damage

Penance is closely connected with reconciliation. Reconciliation with God, with oneself and with others implies overcoming that radical break which is sin. And this is achieved only through the interior transformation or conversion which bears fruit in a person's life through acts of penance....

Sacred Scripture speaks to us of this reconciliation, inviting us to make every effort to attain it. But Scripture also tells us that it is above all a merciful gift of God to humanity. The history of salvation... is the wonderful history of a reconciliation: the reconciliation whereby God, as Father, in the blood and the cross of his Son made man, reconciles the world to himself. He thus brings into being a new family of those who have been reconciled.

Reconciliation becomes necessary because there has been the break of sin from which derive all the other forms of break within man and about him. Reconciliation, therefore, in order to be complete necessarily requires liberation from sin, which is to be rejected in its deepest roots. Thus a close internal link unites conversion and reconciliation. It is impossible to split these two realities or to speak of one and say nothing of the other.

35

An Authentic Witness of the Gospel

John Duns Scotus was called "blessed" almost immediately after his death, which occurred in Cologne on November 8, 1308....

In our age, although it has a wealth of human, scientific and technological resources, many have lost the sense of faith and lead a life distant from Christ and his gospel. Blessed Duns Scotus presents himself to us with his sharp mind and extraordinary ability to penetrate the mystery of God. He also demonstrates the persuasive power of his holiness which for the church and the whole of humanity makes him a teacher of thought and life. Pope Paul VI said that his doctrine "can yield shining arms for combating and chasing away the dark clouds of atheism which casts its shadow upon our era."[16] It energetically builds up the church, sustaining her in her urgent mission of the new evangelization of the peoples of the earth....

Blessed Duns Scotus is an example of fidelity to the revealed truth, of effective priestly ministry, of serious dialogue in search for unity.... John Gerson said that throughout his life Duns Scotus was always motivated "not by the contentious singularity of winning, but by the humility of reaching an accord."[17]

May his spirit and memory enlighten with the very light of Christ the trials and hopes of our society.

❧36❧

Work and Rest

We ought to imitate God both in working and also in resting, since God himself wished to present his own creative activity under the form of work and rest. This activity by God in the world always continues, as the words of Christ attest: "My Father is working still..." (Jn 5:17). He works with creative power by sustaining in existence the world that he called into being from nothing. He works with salvific power in the hearts of those who from the beginning he has destined for "rest" in union with himself in his "Father's house."

Therefore our work, too, not only requires a rest every "seventh day," but also cannot consist in the mere exercise of human strength in external action. Work must leave room for man to prepare himself, by becoming more and more what in the will of God he ought to be, for the "rest" that the Lord reserves for his servants and friends.

❧37❧

The Redeeming Power of Work

Sweat and toil... present the Christian and everyone who is called to follow Christ with the possibility of sharing lovingly in the work that Christ came to do. This work of salvation came about through suffering and death on a cross. By enduring the toil of work in union with Christ crucified for us, man in a way collaborates with the Son of God for the redemption of humanity. He shows himself a true disciple of Christ by carrying the cross in his turn every day in the activity that he is called upon to perform....

The Christian finds in human work a small part of the cross of Christ and accepts it in the same spirit of redemption in which Christ accepted his cross for us. In work, thanks to the light that penetrates us from the resurrection of Christ, we always find a glimmer of new life, of the new good. It is as if it were an announcement of "the new heavens and the new earth" (see 2 Pt 3:13) in which man and the world participate precisely through the toil that goes with work. Through toil—and never without it....

Let the Christian who listens to the word of the living God, uniting work with prayer, know the place that his work has not only in earthly progress but also in the development of the Kingdom of God.

Senior Citizens' Valuable Service

The church stresses with particular joy that senior citizens... have their place and use in the Christian community. They continue to be full members of the community. They are called to contribute as far as they can to its development with their witness, prayer, and also their activities.

The church knows well that many people draw close to God particularly in the so-called "third age." Precisely in this period they can be helped to rejuvenate their spirit through reflection and sacramental life. The experience accumulated in the course of the years leads the elderly person to understand the limits of worldly things and to feel a deeper need for the presence of God in his earthly life. The disappointments they have known in some circumstances have taught them to put their trust in God. Their acquired wisdom can be a great advantage not only to their relatives, but to the whole Christian community.

❧39❧

A Covenant Between Generations

Special attention must be given to the elderly. While in some cultures older people remain a part of the family with an important and active role, in others the elderly are regarded as a useless burden and are left to themselves....

Neglect of the elderly or their outright rejection are intolerable. Their presence in the family, or at least their closeness to the family in cases where limited living space or other reasons make this impossible, is of fundamental importance in creating a climate of mutual interaction and enriching communication between the different age groups. It is therefore important to preserve, or to reestablish where it has been lost, a sort of "covenant" between generations. In this way parents, in their later years, can receive from their children the acceptance and solidarity which they themselves gave to their children when they brought them into the world. This is required by obedience to the divine commandment to honor one's father and mother (see Ex 20:12; Lv 19:3).

❧40❧

Strength to Love

To imitate and live out the love of Christ is not possible for man by his own strength alone. He becomes capable of this love only by virtue of a gift received. As the Lord Jesus receives the love of his Father, so he in turn freely communicates that love to his disciples: "As the Father has loved me, so have I loved you. Live on in my love" (Jn 15:9).

Love and life according to the gospel cannot be thought of first and foremost as a kind of precept, because what they demand is beyond man's abilities. They are possible only as the result of a gift of God who heals, restores, and transforms the human heart by his grace: "For while the law was given through Moses, grace and truth came through Jesus Christ" (see Jn 1:17). The promise of eternal life is thus linked to the gift of grace, and the gift of the Spirit which we have received is even now the "pledge of our inheritance" (Eph 1:14).

❦41❦

Linking People in Peace

In his address to the United Nations Organization on October 4, 1965, Pope Paul VI stated a profound truth when he said: "Peace, as you know, is not built up only by means of politics or the balance of forces and interests. It is constructed with the mind, with ideas, with works of peace." The products of the mind—ideas—the products of culture, and the creative forces of people are meant to be shared. Strategies of peace which remain on the scientific and technical level and which merely measure out balances and verify controls will never be sufficient for real peace unless bonds that link peoples to one another are forged and strengthened. Build up the links that unite people together. Build up the means that will enable peoples and nations to share their culture and values with one another. Put aside all the narrow interests that leave one nation at the mercy of another economically, socially, or politically....

The building of links among peoples means the rediscovery and reassertion of all the values that reinforce peace and that join people together in harmony. This also means the renewal of what is best in the heart of man, the heart that seeks the good of the other in friendship and love.

❧42❧

Terrorism Is Never Justifiable

Another painful wound in today's world is the phenomenon of terrorism. It is understood as the intention to kill people and destroy property indiscriminately, and to create a climate of terror and insecurity, often including the taking of hostages. Even when some ideology or the desire to create a better society is adduced as the motivation for this inhuman behavior, acts of terrorism are never justifiable. Even less so when, as happens today, such decisions and such actions, which at times lead to real massacres and to the abduction of innocent people who have nothing to do with the conflicts, claim to have a propaganda purpose for furthering a cause. It is still worse when they are an end in themselves, so that murder is committed merely for the sake of killing. In the face of such horror and suffering, the words I spoke some years ago are still true, and I wish to repeat them again: "What Christianity forbids is to seek solutions... by the ways of hatred, by the murdering of defenseless people, by the methods of terrorism."[18]

❧43❧

Faith Is No Private Matter

All baptized persons are called by Christ to become his apostles in their own personal situation and in the world: "As the Father has sent me, so I send you" (Jn 20:21). Through his church Christ entrusts you with the fundamental mission of sharing with others the gift of salvation. He invites you to participate in building his kingdom. He chooses you, in spite of the personal limitations everyone has, because he loves you and believes in you. This unconditional love of Christ should be the very soul of your apostolic work, in accord with the words of St. Paul, "The love of Christ impels us" (2 Cor 5:14).

Being disciples of Christ is not a private matter. On the contrary, the gift of faith must be shared with others. For this reason the same apostle writes, "Preaching the gospel is not the subject of a boast; I am under compulsion and have no choice. I am ruined if I do not preach it!" (1 Cor 9:16). Moreover, do not forget that faith is strengthened and grows precisely when it is given to others.

❧44❧

Jesus Is the Answer

Do not be afraid of presenting Christ to someone who does not yet know him. Christ is the true answer, the most complete answer to all the questions which concern the human person and his destiny. Without Christ, the human person remains an unsolvable riddle. Therefore, have the courage to present Christ! Certainly, you must do this in a way which respects each person's freedom of conscience, but you must do it. Helping a brother or sister to discover Christ—the way, the truth, and the life (see Jn 14:6)—is a true act of love for one's neighbor.

It is not an easy task to speak of God today. Many times one finds a wall of indifference and even a certain hostility. How many times will you be tempted to repeat with the prophet Jeremiah, "Ah, Lord God, I know not how to speak; I am too young." But God will always answer, "Say not, 'I am too young.' To whomever I send you, you shall go" (Jer 1:6-7). So, do not be discouraged because you are never alone. The Lord will not fail to accompany you, as he promised, "Know that I am with you always, until the end of the world!" (Mt 28:20).

❧45❧

Neighbors to Everyone

As disciples of Jesus, we are called to become neighbors to everyone (see Lk 10:29-37), and to show special favor to those who are poorest, most alone, and most in need. In helping the hungry, the thirsty, the foreigner, the naked, the sick, the imprisoned—as well as the child in the womb and the old person who is suffering or near death—we have the opportunity to serve Jesus. He himself said: "As often as you did it for one of my least brothers, you did it for me" (Mt 25:40). Hence we cannot but feel called to account and judged by the ever relevant words of St. John Chrysostom: "Do you wish to honor the body of Christ? Do not neglect it when you find it naked. Do not do it homage here in the church with silk fabrics only to neglect it outside where it suffers cold and nakedness."[19]

No Goodness without God

Jesus says [to the rich young man]: "Why do you question me about what is good? There is One who is good. If you wish to enter into life, keep the commandments" (see Mt 19:17).

The statement that "there is only one who is good..." brings us back to the "first tablet" of the commandments, which calls us to acknowledge God as the one Lord of all and to worship him alone for his infinite holiness (see Ex 20:2-11). The good is belonging to God, obeying him, walking humbly with him in doing justice and in loving kindness (see Mi 6:8). Acknowledging the Lord as God is the very core, the heart of the law, from which the particular precepts flow and toward which they are ordered. In the morality of the commandments the fact that the people of Israel belong to the Lord is made evident, because God alone is the one who is good....

But if God alone is the good, no human effort, not even the most rigorous observance of the commandments, succeeds in "fulfilling" the law, that is, acknowledging the Lord as God and rendering him the worship due to him alone (see Mt 4:10). This "fulfillment" can come only from a gift of God: the offer of a share in the divine goodness revealed and communicated in Jesus, the one whom the rich young man addresses with the words "good teacher" (Mk 10:17; Lk 18:18).

✌47✌

Hearts Open to the Spirit

The proclamation of the word of God has Christian conversion as its aim: a complete and sincere adherence to Christ and his gospel through faith. Conversion is a gift of God, a work of the Blessed Trinity. It is the Spirit who opens people's hearts so that they can believe in Christ and "confess him" (see 1 Cor 12:3); of those who draw near to him through faith Jesus says: "No one can come to me unless the Father who sent me draws him" (Jn 6:44).

From the outset, conversion is expressed in faith which is total and radical, and which neither limits nor hinders God's gift. At the same time, it gives rise to a dynamic and lifelong process which demands a continual turning away from "life according to the flesh" to "life according to the Spirit" (see Rom 8:3-5). Conversion means accepting, by a personal decision, the saving sovereignty of Christ and becoming his disciple.

Your Choice: Virtue or Vice

There already exists in man, as a being made up of body and spirit, a certain tension, a certain struggle of tendencies between the "spirit" and the "flesh." But this struggle in fact belongs to the heritage of sin, is a consequence of sin and at the same time a confirmation of it. This is part of everyday experience. As the apostle Paul writes, "Now the works of the flesh are plain: fornication, impurity, licentiousness... drunkenness, carousing and the like." These are the sins that could be called "carnal." But he also adds others: "enmity, strife, jealousy, anger, selfishness, dissension, party spirit, envy" (see Gal 5:19-21). All of this constitutes "works of the flesh."

But with these works, which are undoubtedly evil, Paul contrasts "the fruit of the spirit," such as "love, joy, peace, patient endurance, kindness, generosity, faith, mildness, and chastity" (Gal 5:22-23). From the context it is clear that for the apostle it is not a question of discriminating against and condemning the body, which with the spiritual soul constitutes man's nature and personal subjectivity. Rather, he is concerned with the morally good or bad works, or better the permanent dispositions—virtues and vices—which are the fruit of submission to (in the first case) or of resistance to (in the second case) the saving action of the Holy Spirit. Consequently the apostle writes: "Since we live by the spirit, let us follow the spirit's lead" (Gal 5:25).

St. Francis of Assisi—Instrument of Peace

One of the inspired messages that St. Francis lived out in depth, and which he continues to make resound in the consciences of modern men, is his urgent and fervent desire for peace.

After wholeheartedly choosing the vocation to which God called him, he and his first followers went through the cities, through the villages. They stopped in the squares and neighborhoods where he used to repeat the simple but sublime words, "Peace and good." These words were intended to be not just a desire but also a commitment that should involve his listeners, often rended by divisions and bitter struggle....

St. Francis was a builder and an architect of reconciliation and peace: "The Lord revealed to me," he says, "the greeting we were to use, saying: May the Lord give you peace."[20] His biographer Thomas of Celano portrays thus the actions of the "Poverello": "In all of his sermons, before communicating the word of God to the people, he expressed the desire for peace saying: 'May the Lord give you peace!' This peace he announced always sincerely to men and women, to all he met or all who came to him. In this way he often succeeded, through the grace of the Lord, in making men who were the enemies of peace or of their own salvation become sons of peace and desirous of eternal salvation."[21]

❧50❧

Entrusted to Mary

"Seeing his mother there with the disciple whom he loved, Jesus said to his mother, 'Woman, there is your son.' In turn he said to the disciple, There is your mother.' From that hour onward, the disciple took her into his own home..." (see Jn 19: 25- 27).

These... words fully show the reason for the Marian dimension of the life of Christ's disciples. This is true not only of John, who at that hour stood at the foot of the cross together with his Master's mother, but it is also true of every disciple of Christ, of every Christian. The Redeemer entrusts his mother to the disciple, and at the same time he gives her to him as his mother. Mary's motherhood, which becomes man's inheritance, is a gift: a gift which Christ himself makes personally to every individual. The Redeemer entrusts Mary to John because he entrusts John to Mary. At the foot of the cross there begins that special entrusting of humanity to the mother of Christ, which in the history of the church has been practiced and expressed in different ways....

The Marian dimension of the life of a disciple of Christ is expressed in a special way precisely through this filial entrusting to the mother of Christ, which began with the testament of the Redeemer on Golgotha. Entrusting himself to Mary in a filial manner, the Christian, like the apostle John, "welcomes" the mother of Christ "into his own home" and brings her into everything that makes up his inner life.

Love Knows No Enemies

A stranger is no longer a stranger for the person who must become a neighbor to someone in need, to the point of accepting responsibility for his life, as the parable of the Good Samaritan shows so clearly (see Lk 10:25-37). Even an enemy ceases to be an enemy for the person who is obliged to love him (see Mt 5:38-48; Lk 6:27-35), to "do good" to him (see Lk 6:27, 33, 35) and to respond to his immediate needs promptly and with no expectation of repayment (see Lk 6:34-35). The height of this love is to pray for one's enemy. By so doing we achieve harmony with the providential love of God: "My command to you is: love your enemies, pray for your persecutors. This will prove that you are sons of your heavenly Father, for his sun rises on the bad and the good, he rains on the just and the unjust" (Mt 5:44-45; see Lk 6:28, 35).

Thus the deepest element of God's commandment to protect human life is the requirement to show reverence and love for every person and the life of every person. This is the teaching which the apostle Paul, echoing the words of Jesus, addresses to the Christians in Rome: "The commandments... are all summed up in this, 'You shall love your neighbor as yourself.' Love never does any wrong to the neighbor, hence love is the fulfillment of the law" (Rom 13:9-10).

❧52❧

The Lord Comforts Women
Who Have Had Abortions

I would now like to say a special word to women who have had an abortion. The church is aware of the many factors which may have influenced your decision, and she does not doubt that in many cases it was a painful and even shattering decision. The wound in your heart may not yet have healed. Certainly what happened was and remains terribly wrong. But do not give in to discouragement and do not lose hope. Try rather to understand what happened and face it honestly.

If you have not already done so, give yourselves over with humility and trust to repentance. The Father of mercies is ready to give you his forgiveness and his peace in the sacrament of reconciliation. You will come to understand that nothing is definitively lost and you will also be able to ask forgiveness from your child, who is now living in the Lord. With the friendly and expert help and advice of other people, and as a result of your own painful experience, you can be among the most eloquent defenders of everyone's right to life. Through your commitment to life, whether by accepting the birth of other children or by welcoming and caring for those most in need of someone to be close to them, you will become promoters of a new way of looking at human life.

❧53❧

Faith in Action

What does it mean, then, to be a Christian? It means to continue to receive and accept the witness of the apostles, the eyewitnesses of our salvation. It means to believe in Christ with the same faith that was born in them from the works and the words of the risen Lord.

This is what the Apostle John writes: "The way we can be sure of our knowledge of him is to keep his commandments. The man who claims, 'I know him,' without keeping his commandments, is a liar; in such a one there is no truth. But whoever keeps his word, truly has the love of God been made perfect in him" (1 Jn 2:3-5).

The apostle is speaking of a living faith. Faith is living when it bears the fruit of good works. These are the works of love. Faith is alive through God's love in us. Love is expressed in the observance of the commandments. There can be no contradictions between the knowledge of "I know him" and the actions of one who confesses Christ. Only he who completes his faith with good works remains in the truth.

❧54❧

A Good Father Is a Lover

Authentic conjugal love presupposes and requires that a man have a profound respect for the equal dignity of his wife: "You are not her master," writes St. Ambrose, "but her husband; she was not given to you to be your slave, but your wife…. Reciprocate her attentiveness to you and be grateful for her love."[22] With his wife a man should live "a very special form of personal friendship."[23] As for the Christian, he is called upon to develop a new attitude of love, manifesting toward his wife a charity that is both gentle and strong, like that which Christ has for the church.

Love for his wife as mother of their children and love for the children themselves are for the man the natural way of understanding and fulfilling his own fatherhood. Above all where social and cultural conditions so easily encourage a father to be less concerned with his family or at any rate less involved in the work of education, efforts must be made to restore socially the conviction that the place and task of the father in and for the family is of unique and irreplaceable importance.

How Families Show Concern

Note must be taken of the ever greater importance in our society of hospitality in all its forms, from opening the door of one's home, and still more of one's heart, to the pleas of one's brothers and sisters, to concrete efforts to ensure that every family has its own home as the natural environment that preserves it and makes it grow. In a special way the Christian family is called upon to listen to the apostle's recommendation, "Practice hospitality," (see Rom 12:13) and therefore, imitating Christ's example and sharing in his love, welcome the brother or sister in need....

The social role of families is called upon to find expression also in the form of political intervention: Families should be the first to take steps to see that the laws and institutions of the state not only do not offend, but support and positively defend the rights and duties of the family. Along these lines, families should grow in the awareness of being "protagonists" of what is known as "family politics" and assume responsibility for transforming society; otherwise families will be the first victims of the evils that they have done no more than note with indifference.

❧56❧

Holy Spirit-Inspired Witnesses

When carrying out her mission of giving catechesis, the church—and also every individual Christian devoting himself to that mission within the church and in her name —must be very much aware of acting as a living, pliant instrument of the Holy Spirit. To invoke this Spirit constantly, to be in communion with him, to endeavor to know his authentic inspiration must be the attitude of the teaching church and of every catechist.

Secondly, the deep desire to understand better the Spirit's action and to entrust oneself to Him more fully... must bring about a catechetical awakening. For "renewal in the spirit" will be authentic and will have real fruitfulness in the church, not so much according as it gives rise to extraordinary charisms, but according as it leads the greatest possible number of the faithful, as they travel their daily paths, to make a humble, patient and persevering effort to know the mystery of Christ better and better, and to bear witness to it.

The Dignity of Disabled Persons

In spite of the limitations and sufferings affecting their bodies and faculties, [people with disabilities] point up more clearly the greatness and dignity of man.... They should be helped to participate in the life of society in all its aspects and at all levels accessible to their capacities. The disabled person is one of us and participates fully in the same humanity that we possess. It would be radically unworthy of man, and a denial of our common humanity, to admit to the life of the community, and thus to work, only those who are fully functional. To do so would be to practice a serious form of discrimination, that of the strong and healthy against the weak and sick....

The various bodies involved in the world of labor, both the direct and the indirect employer, should therefore by means of effective and appropriate measures foster the right of disabled people to professional training and work, so that they can be given a productive activity suited to them.

❧58❧

Another Name for Love

What else, then, does the cross of Christ say to us, the cross that in a sense is the final word of his messianic message and mission?... That cross... speaks and never ceases to speak of God the Father, who is absolutely faithful to his eternal love for man, since he "so loved the world"—therefore man in the world—that "he gave his only Son, that whoever believes in him should not perish but have eternal life" (see Jn 3:16). Believing in the crucified Son means "seeing the Father" (see Jn 14:9), means believing that love is present in the world and that this love is more powerful than any kind of evil in which individuals, humanity or the world are involved. Believing in this love means believing in mercy. For mercy is an indispensable dimension of love; it is as it were love's second name.

❧59❧

The Mercy of Justice

Christ emphasizes so insistently the need to forgive others that when Peter asked him how many times he should forgive his neighbor he answered with the symbolic number of "seventy times seven" (Mt 18:22), meaning that he must be able to forgive everyone every time. It is obvious that such a generous requirement of forgiveness does not cancel out the objective requirements of justice. Properly understood, justice constitutes, so to speak, the goal of forgiveness. In no passage of the gospel message does forgiveness, or mercy as its source, mean indulgence toward evil, toward scandals, toward injury or insult. In any case, reparation for evil and scandal, compensation for injury, and satisfaction for insult are conditions for forgiveness. Thus the fundamental structure of justice always enters into the sphere of mercy. Mercy, however, has the power to confer on justice a new content, which is expressed most simply and fully in forgiveness.

❧60❧

Urged to Love

Those who live "by the flesh" experience God's law as a burden and indeed as a denial or at least a restriction of their own freedom. On the other hand, those who are impelled by love and "walk by the Spirit" (see Gal 5:26), and who desire to serve others, find in God's law the fundamental and necessary way in which to practice love as something freely chosen and freely lived out. Indeed, they feel an interior urge—a genuine "necessity" and no longer a form of coercion—not to stop at the minimum demands of the law, but to live them in their "fullness." This is a still uncertain and fragile journey as long as we are on earth, but it is one made possible by grace, which enables us to possess the full freedom of the children of God (see Rom 8:21) and thus to live our moral life in a way worthy of our sublime vocation as "sons in the Son."

❖61❖

A Christian Is a Living Gospel

Every Christian—as he explores the historical record of Scripture and tradition and comes to a deep, abiding faith—experiences that Christ is the risen one and that he is therefore the eternally living one. It is a deep, life-changing experience. No true Christian can keep it hidden as a personal matter. For such an encounter with the living God cries out to be shared—like the light that shines, like the yeast that leavens the whole mass of dough.

The true Christian is a living gospel. That does not mean he is a disciple of a doctrine that is far away in time and foreign to the reality of life. He does not repeat powerless formulas. No, he is convinced and tenacious in asserting the relevance of Christ and the unceasing newness of the gospel. He is always eager before anyone and at any time to give reason for the hope which he harbors in his heart (see 1 Pt 3:15).

Don't Neglect Penance

For a Christian the sacrament of penance is the ordinary way of obtaining forgiveness and the remission of serious sin committed after baptism. Certainly the Savior and his salvific action are not so bound to a sacramental sign as to be unable... to work outside and above the sacraments. But in the school of faith we learn that the same Savior desired and provided that the simple and precious sacraments of faith would ordinarily be the effective means through which his redemptive power passes and operates. It would therefore be foolish, as well as presumptuous, to wish arbitrarily to disregard the means of grace and salvation which the Lord has provided and, in the specific case, to claim to receive forgiveness while doing without the sacrament which was instituted by Christ precisely for forgiveness.

The renewal of the rites carried out after the Second Vatican Council does not sanction any illusion or alteration in this direction. According to the church's intention, it was and is meant to stir up in each one of us a new impulse toward the renewal of our interior attitude; toward a deeper understanding of the nature of the sacrament of penance; toward a reception of the sacrament which is more filled with faith, not anxious but trusting; toward a more frequent celebration of the sacrament which is seen to be completely filled with the Lord's merciful love.

63

Run the Race to Win

Through sports, we value the body. We achieve the best physical condition possible, with remarkable results that bring great satisfaction. From our Christian faith, we know that, by baptism, the human person in his totality and wholeness of body and soul becomes a temple of the Holy Spirit: "You must know that your body is a temple of the Holy Spirit, who is within—the Spirit you have received from God. You are not your own. You have been purchased, and at a price. So glorify God in your body" (1 Cor 6:19-20).

Sports involve a struggle to win a contest and achieve some goal. But from our Christian faith we know that the "incorruptible crown" of eternal life is more valuable than any earthly prize. It is God's gift but it is also the result of a daily conquest in the exercise of virtue. And this is a really important contest according to Paul. He tells us: "Set your hearts on the greater gifts" (1 Cor 12:31). Paul is telling us to set our hearts on the gifts that advance God's kingdom. Those gifts will reap a reward that will have eternal benefits for us if we persevere in running the race.

Safe in the Good Shepherd's Care

In biblical times, the shepherd was not just a leader but a friendly and attentive guardian. He was concerned about the life of his flock. He led the flock to the pastures and springs. He protected it from predators and wild animals. He guarded it from dangers.

The shepherd is a savior. It is easy to trust in him with a simple heart—as we must now do with Christ—because his care provides safety and abundance of life. It is easy to grasp in him the authority and sovereignty of God, who takes the initiative. Extending goodness and grace, he is concerned for us and becomes our steadfast support. Yes, we are his. He made us. We are his people. We are the flock he tends. Christ calls his disciples "mine," because "my Father ... has given them to me" (Jn 10:29, RSV).

Every believer has been given to the Son by the Father in a special way. The Son himself has become a human being to take on the Father's shepherding concern for his flock. A shepherd's concern is synonymous with God's fatherly providence in the Scripture. This providence becomes a living reality for us through the Son, through the Christ.

❧65❧

Miracles of Spiritual Healing

Jesus showed his compassion for the sick and the infirm, revealing his great kindness and tenderness of heart. He was also prepared to save those suffering in soul and body by means of his power to work miracles. He therefore worked many cures, so many that the sick flocked to him to benefit from his miraculous power....

In his dedication to freeing those who approached him from the burden of sickness or infirmity, Jesus allows us to glimpse the special intention of God's mercy in their regard: God is not indifferent to the sufferings caused by disease. He offers his help to the sick through the saving plan that the incarnate Word reveals and fulfills in the world.

Indeed Jesus considers and treats the sick and infirm in the light of the saving work he was sent to accomplish. Bodily cures are part of this work of salvation. At the same time, they are signs of the great spiritual healing he brings humanity. This loftier intention of his emerges clearly when he first forgives the sins of a paralytic, brought before him to be cured....

In this case and in many others, Jesus wants to show by a miracle his power of freeing the human soul from its sins and purifying it. He cures the sick in view of this superior gift, which he offers to all men: in other words, spiritual salvation.

❧66❧

Longing for the Spirit

The present-day church seems to repeat with even greater fervor and with holy insistence: "Come, Holy Spirit! Come! Heal our wounds, our strength renew; On our dryness pour Your dew; Wash the stains of guilt away; Bend the stubborn heart and will; Melt the frozen, warm the chill; Guide the steps that go astray...."[24]

This invocation addressed to the Spirit to obtain the Spirit is really a constant self-insertion into the full magnitude of the mystery of the redemption.... Christ, united with the Father and with each person, continually communicates to us the Spirit who places within us the sentiments of the Son and directs us toward the Father. Our time is particularly hungry for the Spirit because it is hungry for justice, peace, love, goodness, fortitude, responsibility, and human dignity. This is why the church.... must concentrate and gather around that mystery, finding in it the light and the strength that are indispensable for her mission.

❧67❧

The Grounds for Christian Unity

To the people of our time, so sensitive to the proof of concrete living witness, the church is called upon to give an example of reconciliation particularly within herself. And for this purpose we must all work to bring peace to people's minds, to reduce tensions, to overcome divisions and to heal wounds that may have been inflicted by brother on brother.... We must try to be united in what is essential for Christian faith and life, in accordance with the ancient maxim: In what is doubtful, freedom; in what is necessary, unity; in all things, charity.

It is in accordance with this same criterion that the church must conduct her ecumenical activity. For in order to be completely reconciled, she knows that she must continue the quest for unity among those who are proud to call themselves Christians but who are separated from one another, also as churches or communions, and from the church of Rome. The latter seeks a unity which, if it is to be the fruit and expression of true reconciliation, is meant to be based neither upon a disguising of the points that divide nor upon compromises which are as easy as they are superficial and fragile. Unity must be the result of a true conversion of everyone, the result of mutual forgiveness, of theological dialogue and fraternal relations, of prayer and of complete docility to the action of the Holy Spirit, who is also the Spirit of reconciliation.

Free to Choose Christ

The urgency of missionary activity derives from the radical newness of life brought by Christ and lived by his followers. This new life is a gift from God, and people are asked to accept and develop it, if they wish to realize the fullness of their vocation in conformity to Christ....

God offers humanity this newness of life. "Can one reject Christ and everything that he has brought about in the history of humankind? Of course one can. Man is free. He can say no to God...."[25]

Proclaiming Christ and bearing witness to him, when done in a way that respects consciences, does not violate freedom. Faith demands a free adherence on the part of man. But at the same time faith must also be offered to him. As Pope Paul VI said, "Multitudes have the right to know the riches of the mystery of Christ—riches in which we believe the whole of humanity can find, in unsuspected fullness, everything that it is gropingly searching for concerning God, man and his destiny, life and death and truth."[26]

The Eucharist Nourishes the Family

The Eucharist is truly a wondrous sacrament. In it Christ has given us himself as food and drink, as a source of saving power. He has left himself to us that we might have life and have it in abundance (see Jn 10:10).... The life that comes from Christ is a life for us.

It is for you, dear husbands and wives, parents and families! Did Jesus not institute the Eucharist in a family-like setting during the Last Supper? When you meet for meals and are together in harmony, Christ is close to you. And he is Emmanuel, God with us, in an even greater way whenever you approach the table of the Eucharist. It can happen, as it did at Emmaus, that he is recognized only in "the breaking of the bread" (Lk 24:35). It may well be that he is knocking at the door for a long time, waiting for it to be opened so that he can enter and eat with us (see Rv 3:20).

The Last Supper and the words he spoke there contain all the power and wisdom of the sacrifice of the cross. No other power and wisdom exist by which we can be saved and through which we can help to save others. There is no other power and no other wisdom by which you, parents, can educate both your children and yourselves. The educational power of the Eucharist has been proved down the generations and centuries.

❧70❧

Science and the Mystery of Life

The enlightened copyist who in the thirteenth century—as evidenced by the valuable document preserved in the Vatican Library—wished to transcribe the Hippocratic Oath by arranging the text in the form of a cross certainly recognized that rational argumentation on the right to life had value as a preparation for the Christian conception of the human person and the sacredness of life—indeed, for full recognition of the mystery of life. Such recognition does not humiliate or circumscribe the impetus of science, but spurs it on and ennobles it.

❧71❧

A Move Back to the Mercy of God

The present-day mentality, more perhaps than that of people in the past, seems opposed to a God of mercy. In fact, it tends to exclude from life and to remove from the human heart the very idea of mercy. The word and the concept of "mercy" seem to cause uneasiness in man, who, thanks to the enormous development of science and technology never before known in history, has become the master of the earth and has subdued and dominated it (see Gn 1:28). This dominion over the earth... seems to leave no room for mercy....

The truth, revealed in Christ, about God the "Father of mercies," (2 Cor 1:3) enables us to "see" him as particularly close to man, especially when man is suffering, when he is under threat at the very heart of his existence and dignity. And this is why, in the situation of the church and the world today, many individuals and groups guided by a lively sense of faith are turning, I would say almost spontaneously, to the mercy of God. They are certainly being moved to do this by Christ himself, who through his Spirit works within human hearts.

Jesus, Rich in Mercy

Before his own townspeople in Nazareth, Christ refers to the words of the prophet Isaiah: "The Spirit of the Lord is upon me, because he has anointed me to preach good news to the poor..." (see Lk 4:18-19).

Especially through his lifestyle and through his actions, Jesus revealed that love is present in the world in which we live—an effective love, a love that addresses itself to man and embraces everything that makes up his humanity. This love makes itself particularly noticed in contact with suffering, injustice and poverty—in contact with the whole historical "human condition," which in various ways manifests man's limitation and frailty, both physical and moral. It is precisely the mode and sphere in which love manifests itself that in biblical language is called "mercy."

Christ then reveals God who is Father, who is "love." ...Christ reveals God as "rich in mercy," as we read in St. Paul (Eph 2:4). This truth is not just the subject of a teaching. It is a reality made present to us by Christ. Making the Father present as love and mercy is, in Christ's own consciousness, the fundamental touchstone of his mission as the Messiah. This is confirmed by the words that he uttered first in the synagogue at Nazareth and later in the presence of his disciples and of John the Baptist's messengers.

❧73❧

Liberation and Healing

The liberation and salvation brought by the kingdom of God come to the human person both in his physical and spiritual dimensions. Two gestures are characteristic of Jesus' mission: healing and forgiving. Jesus' many healings clearly show his great compassion in the face of human distress, but they also signify that in the kingdom there will no longer be sickness or suffering, and that his mission, from the very beginning, is meant to free people from these evils. In Jesus' eyes, healings are also a sign of spiritual salvation—liberation from sin. By performing acts of healing, he invites people to faith, conversion and the desire for forgiveness (see Lk 5:24). Once there is faith, healing is an encouragement to go further: it leads to salvation (see Lk 18:42-43). The acts of liberation from demonic possession—the supreme evil and symbol of sin and rebellion against God—are signs that indeed "the reign of God has overtaken you" (Mt 12:28).

❧74❧

Toward More Humane Health Care

In my apostolic trips, especially to developing nations, I have seen that health care is a place of struggle for man. For example, technology tends to demand more attention, yet it does not always safeguard the person's rights.

Suffering, disease, and death are fundamental to human life. We must all work with one another to solve in a human way the problems that such realities entail. Helping the sick one to overcome his sickness with dignity is certainly the service that humankind expects from science, from technology, and from the use of medicine. But this is not possible without a clear vision of the need for absolute respect for the human being. After all, the human is the only creature who transcends material reality because of his spiritual side. This must be our constant point of reference if we really want to avoid consequences in the medical field that could cause great social ills. We must respect the dignity of the human person, including his spiritual side.

Women in Leadership

Though not called to the apostolate of the Twelve, and thereby to the ministerial priesthood, many women nevertheless accompanied Jesus in his ministry and assisted the group of apostles (see Lk 8:2-3); were present at the foot of the cross (see Lk 23:49); assisted at the burial of Christ (see Lk 23:55); received and transmitted the message of resurrection on Easter morn (see Lk 24:1-10); and prayed with the apostles in the cenacle awaiting Pentecost (see Acts 1:14).

From the evidence of the gospel, the church at its origin detached herself from the culture of the time and called women to tasks connected with spreading the gospel. In his letters the apostle Paul even cites by name a great number of women for their various functions in service of the primitive Christian community (see Rom 16:1-15; Phil 4:2-3; Col 4:15 and 1 Cor 11:5; 1 Tim 5:16). "If the witness of the apostles founds the Church," stated Paul VI, "the witness of women contributes greatly toward nourishing the faith of Christian communities."[27]

❧76❧

The Irreplaceable Witness of Women

By following the example of Mary, whom Elizabeth shortly afterward called blessed for her having believed (see Lk 1:45), and recalling that Jesus also requested a profession of faith from Martha before he raised Lazarus (see Jn 11:26), the Christian woman will feel called in a unique way to profess and give witness to the faith.

The church needs resolute, consistent and faithful witnesses who, in the face of widespread doubts and disbelief on many levels in society today, will show in word and deed their commitment to the ever living Christ.

We cannot forget that... on the day of Jesus' resurrection, it was the women who first gave witness to this truth....That moment, too, revealed the more intuitive nature of woman's mind, which makes her more open to the revealed truth, more able to grasp the meaning of events and to accept the gospel message. Down the centuries there have been countless proofs of this ability and this readiness.... Women have a very particular approach to handing on the faith and thus Jesus himself summoned them to evangelize.

Gospel Poverty Makes Us Better

Evangelical poverty is very different from socioeconomic poverty…. The latter has harsh and often tragic characteristics, since it is experienced as a form of coercion. [But] evangelical poverty is chosen freely by the person who intends in this way to respond to Christ's admonition: "None of you can be my disciple if he does not renounce all his possessions" (Lk 14:33).

Such evangelical poverty is the source of peace, since through it the individual can establish a proper relationship with God, with others and with creation. The life of the person who puts himself in this situation thus witnesses to humanity's absolute dependence on God who loves all creatures. [They come to recognize] material goods for what they are: a gift of God for the good of all.

Evangelical poverty… transforms those who accept it. They cannot remain indifferent when faced with the suffering of the poor. Indeed, they feel impelled to share actively with God his preferential love for them. Those who are poor in the gospel sense are ready to sacrifice their resources and their own selves so that others may live. Their one desire is to live in peace with everyone, offering to others the gift of Jesus' peace (see Jn 14:27).

St. Clare Saw Christ in the Poor

Clare's contemplative journey, which culminated in her vision of the King of Glory, begins precisely in her total abandonment to the Spirit of the Lord in the same way as Mary did at the Annunciation. It begins with that spirit of poverty (see Lk 1:48) which empties her of everything but the simplicity of a gaze fixed on God.

For Clare, poverty—which she loved so much and mentioned so often in her writings—is the wealth of the soul. Stripped of its own goods, the soul is... like an empty shell in which God can pour out an abundance of his gifts....

If Catherine of Siena is the saintly woman full of passion for the Blood of Christ; the great St. Teresa is the woman who goes from "mansion" to "mansion" to the threshold of the great King in the Interior Castle; and Therese of the Child Jesus is the one who, in gospel simplicity, travels the little way—Clare is the passionate lover of the poor, crucified Christ, with whom she wants to identify absolutely....

In reality, Clare's whole life was a eucharist. Like Francis, from her cloister she raised up a continual "thanksgiving" to God in her prayer, praise, supplication, intercession, weeping, offering and sacrifice. She accepted everything and offered it to the Father in union with the infinite "thanks" of the only begotten Son, the Child, the Crucified, the risen One, who lives at the right hand of the Father.

Virginity—Spiritual Motherhood

Virginity according to the gospel means renouncing marriage and thus physical motherhood. Nevertheless, the renunciation of this kind of motherhood, a renunciation that can involve great sacrifice for a woman, makes possible a different kind of motherhood—motherhood "according to the spirit" (see Rom 8:4). For virginity does not deprive a woman of her prerogatives.

Spiritual motherhood takes on many different forms.... [It] can express itself as concern for people, especially the most needy: the sick, the handicapped, the abandoned, orphans, the elderly, children, young people, the imprisoned and, in general, people on the margins of society. In this way a consecrated woman finds her Spouse, different and the same in each and every person, according to his very words: "As often as you did it for one of my least brothers, you did it for me" (Mt 25:40). Spousal love always involves a special readiness to be poured out for the sake of those who come within one's range of activity. In marriage this readiness, even though open to all, consists mainly in the love that parents give their children. In virginity this readiness is open to all people, who are embraced by the love of Christ the Spouse.

80

Consumerism and Sex

The lure of the so-called "consumer society" is so strong among young people that they become totally dominated and imprisoned by an individualistic, materialistic and hedonistic interpretation of human existence. Material "well-being," which is so intensely sought after, becomes the one ideal to be striven for in life, a well-being which is to be attained in any way and at any price. There is a refusal of anything that speaks of sacrifice and a rejection of any effort to look for and to practice spiritual and religious values. The all-determining "concern" for having supplants the primacy of being. Consequently, personal and interpersonal values are interpreted and lived not according to the logic of giving and generosity but according to the logic of selfish possession and the exploitation of others.

This is particularly reflected in that outlook on human sexuality according to which sexuality's dignity in service to communion... between persons becomes degraded. Thereby [it is] reduced to nothing more than a consumer good. In this case, many young people undergo an affective experience which, instead of contributing to a harmonious and joyous growth in personality,... becomes a serious psychological and ethical process of turning inward toward self. This situation cannot fail to have grave consequences on them in the future.

🍃81🍃

Pornography and the Family

The proliferation of pornographic literature is only one indication of a broader crisis of moral values affecting contemporary society. Pornography is immoral and ultimately antisocial precisely because it is opposed to the truth about the human person, made in the image and likeness of God. By its very nature, pornography denies the genuine meaning of human sexuality as a God-given gift intended to open individuals to love and to sharing in the creative work of God through responsible procreation. By reducing the body to an instrument for the gratification of the senses, pornography frustrates authentic moral growth and undermines the development of mature and healthy relationships. It leads inexorably to the exploitation of individuals, especially those who are most vulnerable, as is so tragically evident in the case of child pornography....

The family is usually the first to suffer from pornography and its damaging effects on children. Consequently, as the primary cell of society, the family must be the first champion in the battle against this evil.

❧82❧

The Joy of Reconciliation

Make ready the way of the Lord, Clear him a straight path (Lk 3:4).

[John the Baptist's] testimony suggests that to go and meet the Lord it is necessary to create "desert" spaces within us and around us—opportunities to give up what is superfluous, to seek the essential, an atmosphere of silence and prayer.

St. John the Baptist invites us above all to return to God, decisively fleeing sin, which infects the human heart and causes man to lose the joy of meeting the Lord....

It is especially through the sacrament of reconciliation that Christians can experience this, rediscovering the truth of their own existence in the light of God's word. They can taste the joy of being once more at peace with themselves and God.

The Family's Missionary Impulse

Christ himself chose a human family as the place for his incarnation and preparation for the mission entrusted to him by the heavenly Father. Furthermore, he founded a new family, the church, as a continuation of his universal saving action. Church and family, therefore, in view of Christ's mission, have mutual bonds and converging purposes. If all Christians share responsibility for... missionary activity,... then the Christian family, based on a special sacrament, must feel all the more impelled by the missionary spirit....

The two patron saints of the missions, as many gospel workers, had the joy of living their childhood in a truly Christian family. St. Francis Xavier reflected in his missionary life the generosity, loyalty and deep religious spirit which he experienced in his family and especially alongside his mother. St. Teresa of the Child Jesus, for her part, writes with characteristic simplicity: "All my life long the good Lord has surrounded me with love: my earliest memories are filled with the most tender caresses and smiles!"[28]

Common Life, Common Love

The branches are joined to the vine and from it they draw nourishment to make the "fruit" blossom and grow. The disciples are joined to the Lord in the same way....

The branches have no life of their own. They live only if they remain joined to the vine from which they have grown. Their life is identified with that of the vine. A single sap flows between them both; vine and branches bear the same fruit. Thus there is an unbreakable bond between them, which vividly symbolizes the link between Jesus and his disciples: "Live on in me, as I do in you" (Jn 15:4).

In the vine branches are all nourished by the same sap, they are also linked to one another by reciprocal communion. The demand for communion in love derives from this communion of life: "Love one another as I have loved you" (Jn 15:12). It is a strong, unlimited and boundless love. Jesus relates it to his suffering and death to redeem his "friends," the disciples who have believed in him. "There is no greater love than this: to lay down one's life for one's friends" (Jn 15:13). The reference to the redemption highlights even more strongly the common destiny of Christ's disciples. They are all redeemed by *one* Lord."

❧85❧

The Vine and the Bread

"I am the vine.... He who lives in me and I in him, will produce abundantly" (Jn 15:5). Christ remains in us through the Eucharist. Jesus' invitation to "remain in him" reminds us of another truth he mentioned, this time in the context of his great discourse on "the bread of life." "The man who feeds on my flesh and drinks my blood has eternal life" (see Jn 6:56). So Jesus tells the multitudes.

This parallel passage shows us how the symbol of the vine also has eucharistic significance. We see how our remaining in Jesus, the True Vine, is fulfilled by our taking him as our very food. The Eucharist is precisely Jesus who remains in our midst in a true and real way. Even though to us he appears under the sacramental signs of the bread and wine, he is truly present with us.

It is true that these signs do not give us the joy of seeing him with our senses, but they do offer us the assurance of his full presence in our midst. We are the beneficiaries of his ability to be multiplied in all places and at all times sacramentally as food for our souls. Let us all draw near to the table of the Lord to receive this precious food.

The Sacrament and Soul of Love

Eucharistic worship constitutes the soul of all Christian life. In fact, Christian life is expressed in the fulfilling of the greatest commandment—in the love of God and neighbor. This love finds its source in the Blessed Sacrament, which is commonly called the sacrament of love.

The Eucharist signifies this charity, and therefore recalls it, makes it present and at the same time brings it about. Every time that we consciously share in it, there opens in our souls a real dimension of that unfathomable love that includes everything that God has done and continues to do for us human beings. As Christ says: "My Father goes on working and so do I." Together with this unfathomable and free gift... there also springs up within us a lively response of love. We not only know love; we ourselves begin to love. We enter... upon the path of love and along this path make progress....

Eucharistic worship is therefore precisely the expression of that love which is the authentic and deepest characteristic of the Christian vocation.

87

Share the Treasure

To be committed to the new evangelization means that we are convinced that we have something of value to offer to the human family at the dawn of the new millennium.... It is not enough to offer a "merely human wisdom, a pseudoscience of well-being."[29] We must be convinced that we have "a pearl of great price" (see Mt 13:46), a great "treasure" (see Mt 13:44), which is fundamental to the earthly existence and eternal salvation of every member of the human race....

At a time like this, when many are confused regarding the fundamental truths and values on which to build their lives and seek their eternal salvation; when many Catholics are in danger of losing their faith—the pearl of great price; when there are not enough priests, not enough religious sisters and brothers to give support and guidance, not enough contemplative religious to keep before people's eyes the sense of the absolute supremacy of God, we must be convinced that Christ is knocking at many hearts, looking for young people like you to send into the vineyard, where an abundant harvest is ready....

Let us earnestly pray to the Lord of the harvest that the youth of the world will not hesitate to reply: "Here am I! Send me!" "Send us!"

Life Over Death

In the face of the mystery of death people are helpless. Human certitudes begin to waver. However, it is precisely in the face of this setback that Christian faith, if it is understood and accepted in all its richness, offers itself as a source of serenity and peace. In fact, in the light of the gospel the human person assumes a new, supernatural dimension. What seemed to be meaningless acquires sense and value.

When there is no reference to the saving message of faith and hope, the consequence is that the appeal of charity is weakened. Utilitarian and pragmatic principles enter into play which ultimately hold that it is logical and even justifiable to take a life that has become a burden to self or others.... Here we can think, for example, of abortion, euthanasia of premature newborns, suicide, euthanasia of the terminally ill, and the many worrisome interventions in the genetic field....

Especially in regard to the inescapable event of death, the church again and again offers her lasting teaching, valid today as well as in the past, based on the message of Christ.

Life is a gift from the Creator, to be spent in the service of one's brothers and sisters who, in the plan of salvation, can always draw benefit from it. It is, therefore, never licit to harm its course, from its beginning to its natural end. Rather it is to be accepted, respected and promoted with every means available, and defended from every threat.

❧89❧

Nationalism Wounds Christ

We are faced with a new paganism: the deification of the nation. History has shown that the passage from nationalism to totalitarianism is swift and that, when states are no longer equal, people themselves end up by no longer being equal. Thus the natural solidarity between peoples is destroyed, the sense of proportion is distorted, the principle of the unity of mankind is held in contempt.

The Catholic Church cannot accept such a vision of things. Universal by nature, she is conscious of being at the service of all and never identifies with any one national community. She welcomes into her bosom all nation, races and cultures. She is mindful of—indeed she knows that she is the depositary of—God's design for humanity: to gather all people into one family. And this because he is the Creator and Father of all. That is the reason why every time that Christianity—whether according to its Western or Eastern tradition— becomes the instrument of a form of nationalism, it is as it were wounded in its very heart and made sterile.

Exercising Christ's Kingship

Through charity toward one's neighbor, the lay faithful exercise and manifest their participation in the kingship of Christ, that is, in the power of the Son of Man who "has not come to be served but to serve" (Mk 10:45). They live and manifest such a kingship in a most simple yet exalted manner. [This is] possible for everyone at all times because charity is the highest gift offered by the Spirit for the building up of the church (see 1 Cor 13:13) and for the good of humanity....

The same charity, realized not only by individuals but also in a joint way by groups and communities, is and will always be necessary. Nothing and no one will be able to substitute for it, not even the multiplicity of institutions and public initiatives forced to give a response to the needs... of entire populations.... Various forms of volunteer work which express themselves in a multiplicity of services and activities continue to come about and to spread, particularly in organized society. If this impartial service be truly given for the good of all persons, especially the most in need and forgotten by the social services of society itself, then volunteer work can be considered an important expression of the apostolate in which lay men and women have a primary role.

＊91＊

The Promise of Renewal Communities

A rapidly growing phenomenon in the young churches... is that of "ecclesial basic communities" (also known by other names) which are proving to be good centers for Christian formation and missionary outreach. These are groups of Christians, who, at the level of the family or in a similarly restricted setting, come together for prayer, Scripture reading, catechesis, and discussion on human and ecclesial problems with a view to a common commitment. These communities are a sign of vitality within the church, an instrument of formation and evangelization, and a solid starting point for a new society based on a "civilization of love."

These communities decentralize and organize the parish community to which they always remain united. They... become a leaven of Christian life, of care for the poor and neglected and of commitment to the transformation of society. Within them the individual Christian experiences community and therefore senses that he or she is playing an active role and is encouraged to share in the common task. Thus, these communities become a means of evangelization and of the initial proclamation of the gospel, and a source of new ministries. At the same time, by being imbued with Christ's love, they also show how divisions, tribalism and racism can be overcome.

The Limits of Democracy

Democracy cannot be idolized to the point of making it a substitute for morality or a panacea for immorality. Fundamentally, democracy is a "system" and as such is a means and not an end. Its "moral" value is not automatic, but depends on conformity to the moral law to which it, like every other form of human behavior, must be subject: in other words, its morality depends on the morality of the ends which it pursues and of the means which it employs.

If today we see an almost universal consensus with regard to the value of democracy, this is to be considered a positive "sign of the times," as the church's magisterium has frequently noted. But the value of democracy stands or falls with the values which it embodies and promotes. Of course, values such as the dignity of every human person, respect for inviolable and inalienable human rights, and the adoption of the "common good" as the end and criterion regulating political life are certainly fundamental and not to be ignored....

If, as a result of tragic obscuring of the collective conscience, an attitude of skepticism were to succeed in bringing into question even the fundamental principles of the moral law, the democratic system itself would be shaken in its foundations.

❧93❧

The Wellspring of Holiness

"The Spirit of the Lord is upon me" (Lk. 4:18). The Spirit is not simply "upon" the Messiah, but he "fills" him, penetrating every part of him.... Through the Spirit, Jesus belongs totally and exclusively to God. He shares in the infinite holiness of God, who calls him, chooses him and sends him forth. In this way the Spirit of the Lord is revealed as the source of holiness and of the call to holiness.

This same "Spirit of the Lord" is "upon" the entire people of God, which becomes established as a people "consecrated" to God and "sent" by God to announce the gospel of salvation. The members of the people of God are "inebriated" and "sealed" with the Spirit (see 1 Cor. 12:13; 2 Cor. 1:21ff; Eph. 1:13; 4:30) and called to holiness.

In particular, the Spirit reveals to us and communicates the fundamental calling which the Father addresses to everyone from all eternity: the vocation to be "holy and blameless before him... in love," by virtue of our predestination to be his adopted children through Jesus Christ (see Eph. 1:4-5). This is not all. By revealing and communicating this vocation to us, the Spirit becomes within us the principle and wellspring of its fulfillment. He, the Spirit of the Son (see Gal. 4:6), configures us to Christ Jesus and makes us sharers in his life as Son, that is, sharers in his life of love for the Father and for our brothers and sisters.

❧94❧

Seeing God Face to Face

Seeing God face to face is the deepest desire of the human heart. How eloquent are the words of the apostle Philip in this respect when he says: "Lord,... show us the Father and that will be enough for us" (Jn 14:8). Philip's words are eloquent because they bear witness to the deepest thirst and desire of the human spirit. But Jesus' answer is even more eloquent.

Jesus explains to the apostles: "Whoever has seen me has seen the Father" (Jn 14:9). Jesus is the full revelation of the Father. He explains to the world what the Father is like—not because he is the Father—but because he is completely one with the Father in the communion of divine life. In Jesus' own words: "I am in the Father and the Father is in me" (Jn 14:11).

Thanks be to God! Man does not have to seek God all alone anymore. With Christ, man discovers God and discovers him in Christ.

❧95❧

The Suicide of Sin

As a rupture with God, sin is an act of disobedience by a creature who rejects, at least implicitly, the very one from whom he came and who sustains him in life. It is therefore a suicidal act. Since by sinning man refuses to submit to God, his internal balance is also destroyed. It is precisely within himself that contradictions and conflicts arise. Wounded in this way, man almost inevitably causes damage to the fabric of his relationship with others and with the created world. This is an objective law and an objective reality. [It is] verified in so many ways in the human psyche and in the spiritual life as well as in society, where it is easy to see the signs and effects of internal disorder.

The mystery of sin is composed of this twofold wound which the sinner opens in himself and in his relationship with his neighbor. Therefore one can speak of personal and social sin: From one point of view, every sin is personal; from another point of view, every sin is social insofar as and because it also has social repercussions.

The Personal Freedom to Sin

Sin, in the proper sense, is always a personal act, since it is an act of freedom on the part of an individual person and not properly of a group or community. This individual may be conditioned, incited and influenced by numerous and powerful external factors. He may also be subjected to tendencies, defects and habits linked with his personal condition. In not a few cases such external and internal factors may attenuate, to a greater or lesser degree, the person's freedom and therefore his responsibility and guilt.

But it is a truth of faith, also confirmed by our experience and reason, that the human person is free. This truth cannot be disregarded in order to place the blame for individuals' sins on external factors such as structures, systems or other people. Above all, this would be to deny the person's dignity and freedom, which are manifested—even though in a negative and disastrous way—also in this responsibility for sin committed. Hence there is nothing so personal and untransferable in each individual as merit for virtue or responsibility for sin.

A Beacon from Above

Divine providence and human freedom are not opposed to each other. Quite the opposite is true. No, they reveal a communion of love as God respects and works with our free will. For example, as we consider our future destiny, we find in divine revelation—specifically in Christ—a providential light which shows us the way of salvation and the will of the Father.

God accomplishes this, even though he keeps the mystery intact. From such a perspective, divine providence does not deny the presence of evil and suffering in man's life. Far from it! It becomes the bulwark of our hope in time of suffering, and even offers us a glimpse of how we can draw good out of evil.

Let us remember, finally, the great light which Vatican II has shone on God's providence when it refers to the progress of the world that will be ours as the kingdom of God grows, revealing the constancy and the wisdom of our loving God. "Let him who is wise understand these things; let him who is prudent know them. Straight are the paths of the Lord, in them the just walk, but sinners stumble in them" (Hos 14:10).

❧98❧

We Are Our Own Parents

Human acts are moral acts because they express and determine the goodness or evil of the individual who performs them. They do not produce a change merely in the state of affairs outside of man but, to the extent that they are deliberate choices, they give moral definition to the very person who performs them, determining his profound spiritual traits. This was perceptively noted by St. Gregory of Nyssa: "...We are in a certain way our own parents, creating ourselves as we will, by our decisions."[30]

Human Love in God's Image

God created man in his own image and likeness. Calling him to existence through love, he called him at the same time for love.

God is love, and in himself he lives a mystery of personal loving communion. Creating the human race in his own image and continually keeping it in being, God inscribed in the humanity of man and woman the vocation, and thus the capacity and responsibility, of love and communion. Love is therefore the fundamental and innate vocation of every human being....

Christian revelation recognizes two specific ways of realizing the vocation of the human person, in its entirety, to love: marriage and virginity or celibacy. Either one is in its own proper form an actuation of the most profound truth of man, of his being "created in the image of God."

Consequently sexuality, by means of which man and woman give themselves to one another through the acts which are proper and exclusive to spouses, is by no means something purely biological. But [it] concerns the innermost being of the human person as such. It is realized in a truly human way only if it is an integral part of the love by which a man and a woman commit themselves totally to one another until death. The total physical self-giving would be a lie if it were not the sign and fruit of a total personal self-giving.

❧100❧

Forming Children for Life

It is above all in raising children that the family fulfills its mission to proclaim the gospel of life. By word and example, in the daily round of relations and choices, and through concrete actions and signs, parents lead their children to authentic freedom, actualized in the sincere gift of self. And they cultivate in them respect for others, a sense of justice, cordial openness, dialogue, generous service, solidarity and all the other values which help people to live life as a gift.

In raising children Christian parents must be concerned about their children's faith and help them to fulfill the vocation God has given them. The parents' mission as educators also includes teaching and giving their children an example of the true meaning of suffering and death. They will be able to do this if they are sensitive to all kinds of suffering around them and, even more, if they succeed in fostering attitudes of closeness, assistance and sharing toward sick or elderly members of the family.

A High Moral Ideal for Our Youth

A serious moral crisis affects the lives of many young people, leaving them adrift. They are often without hope and are conditioned to look only for instant gratification. Yet everywhere there are young men and women deeply concerned about the world around them. They are ready to give the best of themselves in service to others. They are particularly sensitive to life's transcendent meaning.

But how do we help them? Only by instilling a high moral vision can a society ensure that its young people are given the possibility to mature as free and intelligent human beings. Then they will be endowed with a robust sense of responsibility to the common good. Then they will be capable of working with others to create a community and a nation with a strong moral fiber.

To educate without a value system based on truth is to abandon young people to moral confusion, personal insecurity and easy manipulation. No country, not even the most powerful, can endure if it deprives its own children of this essential good. Respect for the dignity and worth of every person, integrity and responsibility, as well as understanding, compassion and solidarity toward others, survive only if they are passed on in families, in schools and through the communications media.

❧102❧

Trials Strengthen a Marriage

Christ's love is the source and foundation of the love uniting the spouses.... "Husbands, love your wives, as Christ loved the church. He gave himself up for her..." (Eph 5:25).

It must be said over and over again to everyone that, with his absolutely faithful love, Jesus Christ gives Christian spouses the strength of fidelity and enables them to resist the temptation to separate, which today is so widespread and seductive.

We must remember that, since the love of Christ the Bridegroom for the church is a redemptive love, the love of Christian spouses becomes an active participation in redemption.

Redemption is tied to the cross: and this helps us understand and appreciate the meaning of the trials that the couple's life is certainly not spared, but which in God's plan are meant to reinforce their love and bring greater fruitfulness to their married life. Far from promising his married followers an earthly paradise, Jesus Christ offers them the opportunity and the vocation to make a journey with him which, through difficulties and suffering, will strengthen their union and lead them to a greater joy, as proven by the experience of so many Christian couples, in our day as well.

❧103❧

Prayer Makes Families Good

Prayer is the place where, in a very simple way, the creative and fatherly remembrance of God is made manifest: not only man's remembrance of God, but also and especially God's remembrance of man. In this way, the prayer of the family as a community can become a place of common and mutual remembrance: the family is in fact a community of generations.

In prayer everyone should be present: the living and those who have died, and also those yet to come into the world. Families should pray for all of their members, in view of the good which the family is for each individual and which each individual is for the whole family. Prayer strengthens this good, precisely as the common good of the family. Moreover, it creates this good ever anew. In prayer, the family discovers itself as the first "us," in which each member is "I" and "thou"; each member is for the others either husband or wife, father or mother, son or daughter, brother or sister, grandparent or grandchild.

Satisfying Your Deepest Self

"Go to your room, close your door," Jesus instructs us (Mt 6:6). Conversion to God cannot happen in the midst of distraction. Reflection and a clear focus on the Lord are necessary. Man must find his true and highest self and, at the same time, his deepest self.

Why deepest? Why truest and highest? Because this understanding of man relates to his creation and the creation of the world. To all the creatures of the visible world around him, man stands out as lord and master. He is called to subdue all creatures and to have dominion over the earth. This is the first commandment he received from the Creator.

Not only has God made man the crown of creation, God has also shaped man in the depths of his being. Because man is also spirit, he can achieve where the rest of creation falls short. Man's fundamental nature—as both spirit and flesh—does not allow him to find ultimate meaning in mere physical creation.

Man cannot satisfy his deepest self through the visible world. Not even by subduing creation and progressing in his ability to develop, to create, and to discover—can he find true happiness in his inmost being. "What profit would a man show if he were to gain the whole world?" asks Jesus (Mt 16:26). No, man cannot fulfill his deepest self in this way.

Eternal Life Begins Now

The dignity of this life is linked not only to its beginning, to the fact that it comes from God, but also to its final end, to its destiny of fellowship with God in knowledge and love of him....

The love which every human being has for life cannot be reduced simply to a desire to have sufficient space for self-expression and for entering into relationships with others; rather, it develops in a joyous awareness that life can become the "place" where God manifests himself, where we meet him and enter into communion with him. The life which Jesus gives in no way lessens the value of our existence in time; it takes it and directs it to its final destiny: "I am the resurrection and the life.... Whoever is alive and believes in me will never die" (Jn 11:25-26).

TV—to Watch or Not to Watch

Besides being discriminating television viewers themselves, parents should actively help to form in their children viewing habits conducive to sound development, human, moral and religious. Parents should inform themselves in advance about program content and make a conscious choice on that basis for the good of the family—to watch or not to watch. Reviews and evaluations provided by religious agencies and other responsible groups—together with sound media education programs—can be helpful in this regard. Parents should also discuss television with their children, guiding them to regulate the amount and quality of their viewing, and to perceive and judge the ethical values underlying particular programs, because the family is "the privileged means for transmitting the religious and cultural values which help the person to acquire his or her own identity."

Forming children's viewing habits will sometimes mean simply turning off the television set: because there are better things to do, because consideration for other family members requires it, or because indiscriminate television viewing can be harmful. Parents who make regular, prolonged use of television as a kind of electronic baby-sitter surrender their role as the primary educators of their children. Such dependence on television can deprive family members of opportunities to interact with one another through conversation, shared activities and common prayer.

Follow Mary into the Millennium

O**n** the eve of the third millennium the whole church is invited to live more intensely the mystery of Christ by gratefully cooperating in the work of salvation. The church does this together with Mary and following the example of Mary, the church's mother and model: Mary is the model of that maternal love which should inspire all who cooperate in the church's apostolic mission for the rebirth of humanity. Therefore, "strengthened by the presence of Christ, the church journeys through time toward the consummation of the ages and goes to meet the Lord who comes. But on this journey... she proceeds along the path already trodden by the Virgin Mary."[31]

✤108✤

The Fruit of Suffering Is Peace

On the threshold of the third millennium, peace is, unfortunately, still distant…. The identification of the causes and the search for solutions quite often appear laborious. Even among Christians bloody fratricidal struggles are sometimes seen to take place. But those who set about listening to the gospel in an open spirit cannot grow weary of recalling for themselves and others the necessity of forgiveness and reconciliation. They are called to the altar of daily, ardent prayer, together with the sick all over the world, to present the offering of suffering which Christ has accepted as a means to redeem mankind and save it.

The source of peace is the cross of Christ, in which we are all saved…. Peace is the fruit of justice and love, whose summit is the generous offering of one's own suffering, spurred—if necessary—to the point of giving one's life in union with Christ….

To use suffering to advantage and offer it for the salvation of the world are, indeed, themselves an action and mission of peace. From the courageous witness of the weak, the sick and the suffering, the loftiest contribution to peace can flow forth. Suffering, in fact, stimulates deeper spiritual communion, fostering the recovery of a better quality of life, on the one hand, and promoting a convinced commitment to peace among men, on the other.

❧109❧

Solidarity, a Sacrament of Unity

Solidarity is undoubtedly a Christian virtue.... In the light of faith, solidarity seeks to go beyond itself, to take on the specifically Christian dimension of total gratuity, forgiveness and reconciliation. One's neighbor is then not only a human being with his or her own rights and a fundamental equality with everyone else. But [her or she] becomes the living image of God the Father, redeemed by the blood of Jesus Christ and placed under the permanent action of the Holy Spirit. One's neighbor must therefore be loved, even if an enemy, with the same love with which the Lord loves him or her; and for that person's sake one must be ready for sacrifice, even the ultimate one: to lay down one's life for the brethren (see 1 Jn 3:16).

Awareness of the common fatherhood of God, of the brotherhood of all in Christ—"children in the Son"—and of the presence and life-giving action of the Holy Spirit will bring to our vision of the world a new criterion for interpreting it. Beyond human and natural bonds, already so close and strong, there is discerned in the light of faith a new model of the unity of the human race, which must ultimately inspire our solidarity. This supreme model of unity, which is a reflection of the intimate life of God, one God in three Persons, is what we Christians mean by the word "communion." This specifically Christian communion, jealously preserved, extended and enriched with the Lord's help, is the soul of the church's vocation to be a "sacrament," in the senses already indicated.

True Liberation

To the question, "why mission?" we reply with the church's faith and experience that true liberation consists in opening oneself to the love of Christ.... Mission is an issue of faith, an accurate indicator of our faith in Christ and his love for us.

The temptation today is to reduce Christianity to merely human wisdom, a pseudoscience of well-being. In our heavily secularized world a "gradual secularization of salvation" has taken place, so that people strive for the good of man, but man who is truncated, reduced to his merely horizontal dimension.

We know, however, that Jesus came to bring integral salvation, one which embraces the whole person and all humanity, and opens up the wondrous prospect of divine filiation. Why mission? Because to us, as to St. Paul, "was given the grace to preach to the Gentiles the unfathomable riches of Christ" (Eph 3:8). Newness of life in him is the "Good News" for men and women of every age: all are called to it and destined for it. Indeed, all people are searching for it, albeit at times in a confused way, and have a right to know the value of this gift and to approach it freely. The church, and every individual Christian within her, may not keep hidden or monopolize this newness and richness which has been received from God's bounty in order to be communicated to all humankind.

This Mortal Life Is a Most Beautiful Thing

Like the psalmist, we too, in our daily prayer as individuals and as a community, praise and bless God our Father, who knitted us together in our mother's womb, and saw and loved us while we were still without form (see Ps 139:13, 15-16). We exclaim with overwhelming joy: "I give you thanks that I am fearfully, wonderfully made; wonderful are your works. My soul also you knew full well" (Ps 139:14).

Indeed, [as Pope Paul VI said,] "despite its hardships, its hidden mysteries, its suffering and its inevitable frailty, this mortal life is a most beautiful thing, a marvel ever new and moving, an event worthy of being exalted in joy and glory."[32] Moreover, man and his life appear to us not only as one of the greatest marvels of creation: for God has granted to man a dignity which is near to divine (see Ps 8:5-6). In every child which is born and in every person who lives or dies we see the image of God's glory. We celebrate this glory in every human being, a sign of the living God, an icon of Jesus Christ.

The Lord Is Near

The Lord is near! Behold the words of the prophet Zephaniah and be filled with joy: "Shout for joy, O daughter Zion!... The King of Israel, the Lord, is in your midst, you have no further misfortune to fear... Fear not, O Zion, be not discouraged" (Zep 3:14-16).

God's nearness, his presence in the midst of his people Israel, is the source of our strength against all sorts of evil, the prophet tells us. The presence of God is a saving help. He is "a mighty savior" (Zep 3:17). This is the source of the renewal of our spirits. For God's nearness, his presence among men, manifests his love—a love that overcomes evil.

The New Testament bears witness to this truth. For instance, Paul in the Letter to the Philippians tells us "Rejoice in the Lord always! I say it again. Rejoice!... The Lord is near" (Phil 4:4-5). Rejoice in his saving presence and have an unshakable confidence in God. The apostle then writes: "Dismiss all anxiety from your minds. Present your needs to God in every form of prayer and in petitions full of gratitude" (Phil 4:6).

The expression "the Lord is near" is an invitation to intimacy with him, an intimacy that is realized in a direct way through prayer. It is during prayer that we open up ourselves to God and share with him our very lives.

Aggressive Evangelization

Jesus Christ is the stable principle and fixed center of the mission that God himself has entrusted to man. We must all share in this mission and concentrate all our forces on it, since it is more necessary than ever for modern mankind. If this mission seems to encounter greater opposition nowadays than ever before, this shows that today it is more necessary than ever and, in spite of the opposition, more awaited than ever.

Here we touch indirectly on the mystery of the divine "economy" which linked salvation and grace with the cross. It was not without reason that Christ said that "the kingdom of heaven has suffered violence, and the violent take it by force" (Mt 11:12) and moreover that "the worldly take more initiative than the other-worldly" (Lk 16:8). We gladly accept this rebuke, that we may be like those "violent people of God" that we have so often seen in the history of the church and still see today, and that we may consciously join in the great mission of revealing Christ to the world, helping each person to find himself in Christ, and helping the contemporary generations of our brothers and sisters, the peoples, nations, states, mankind, developing countries and countries of opulence—in short, helping everyone to get to know the "unfathomable riches of Christ" (Eph 3:8), since these riches are for every individual and are everybody's property.

🙦114🙤

A Reason for Hope

How can God's all-powerful action fit in with our freedom? And how can our freedom fit in with his unfailing plans? What will our future be like? How can we ever begin to understand and recognize his infinite wisdom and truth in the face of the world's evils? What about the moral evil of sin? What about the suffering of the innocent?

This history of ours—with the rise and fall of nations, with its terrible catastrophes and its sublime acts of greatness and of holiness—what does it all mean? Can it be that a final cataclysm will bury forever all kinds of life? Or else we wonder if there is really a providential and loving being, whom we call God. This God who surrounds us with his intelligence, his tenderness, his wisdom. This God who leads us firmly yet gently. This God who guides our world, our lives, and even our rebellious will, if we yield to him. This God who leads us toward the rest of the "seventh day," the rest of a creation that is nearing its fulfillment.

Here is the answer. The Word stands poised between hope and despair. Yes, the Word of God gives us great reasons for hope. It is ever new, so splendid is the Word of God. It baffles the human mind with its incredible message.

Your Life for Your Friends

He who had come "not... to be served but to serve—to give his life in ransom for the many" (Mk 10:45) attains on the cross the heights of love: "There is no greater love than this: to lay down one's life for one's friends" (Jn 15:13). And he died for us while we were yet sinners (see Rom 5:8).

In this way Jesus proclaims that life finds its center, its meaning and its fulfillment when it is given up.

At this point our meditation becomes praise and thanksgiving, and at the same time urges us to imitate Christ and follow in his footsteps (see 1 Pt 2:21).

We too are called to give our lives for our brothers and sisters, and thus to realize in the fullness of truth the meaning and destiny of our existence.

We shall be able to do this because you, O Lord, have given us the example and have bestowed on us the power of your Spirit. We shall be able to do this if every day, with you and like you, we are obedient to the Father and do his will.

Grant, therefore, that we may listen with open and generous hearts to every word which proceeds from the mouth of God. Thus we shall learn not only to obey the commandment not to kill human life, but also to revere life, to love it and to foster it.

A New Springtime for the Gospel

If we look at today's world, we are struck by many negative factors that can lead to pessimism. But this feeling is unjustified: we have faith in God our Father and Lord, in his goodness and mercy. As the third millennium of the redemption draws near, God is preparing a great springtime for Christianity, and we can already see its first signs. In fact, both in the non-Christian world and in the traditionally Christian world, people are gradually drawing closer to gospel ideals and values, a development which the church seeks to encourage. Today in fact there is a new consensus among peoples about these values: the rejection of violence and war; respect for the human person and for human rights; the desire for freedom, justice and brotherhood; the surmounting of different forms of racism and nationalism; the affirmation of the dignity and role of women.

Christian hope sustains us in committing ourselves fully to the new evangelization and to the worldwide mission, and leads us to pray as Jesus taught us: "Your kingdom come, your will be done on earth as it is in heaven" (Mt 6:10).

Where Can We Find Peace?

The church with her heart, which embraces all human hearts, implores from the Holy Spirit that happiness which only in God has its complete realization: the joy "that no one will be able to take away" (see Jn 16:22), the joy which is the fruit of love, and therefore of God who is love. She implores "the righteousness, the peace and the joy of the Holy Spirit" in which, in the words of St. Paul, "consists the Kingdom of God" (see Rom 14:17; Gal 5:22).

Peace too is the fruit of love: that interior peace, which weary man seeks in his inmost being; that peace besought by humanity, the human family, peoples, nations, continents, anxiously hoping to obtain it in... the transition from the second to the third Christian millennium. Since the way of peace passes in the last analysis through love and seeks to create the civilization of love, the church fixes her eyes on him who is the love of the Father and the Son. And in spite of increasing dangers she does not cease to trust, she does not cease to invoke and to serve the peace of man on earth. Her trust is based on him who, being the Spirit-love, is also the Spirit of peace. He does not cease to be present in our human world, on the horizon of minds and hearts, in order to "fill the universe" with love and peace.

❧118❧

Receive Christ's Gift of Life

Redemption starts with the cross and is accomplished in the resurrection. The Lamb redeemed the sheep. The innocent Christ reconciled sinners to the Father.

Behold, humanity has been released from death and restored to life. Behold, humanity has been set free from sin and restored to love. All of you who are still caught in the darkness of death, listen: Christ is risen! All of you who live under the weight of sin, listen: Christ has conquered sin in his cross and resurrection. Surrender your life to him.

O people of the modern world! Submit yourselves to him and to his power! The more you discover in yourself the old ways of sin, the more you become aware of the horror of death on the horizon of your life, submit yourself all the more to his power to save.

❧119❧

Good News for All

Live in the faith and hand it on to your children. Bear witness to it in your life. Love the church as a mother. Live in her and for her. Make room in your hearts for all men. Forgive one another and be peacemakers wherever you are.

To non-believers, I say: "Seek God, for he is seeking you."

And to those who suffer, I say: "Be confident. For Christ, who has gone before you, will give you strength to face sorrow."

To the youth, I say: "Make a good investment of your life, for it is a precious treasure."

To everyone, I say: "May the grace of God accompany you every day."

And greet your small children in my name, as soon as they wake up. How I would like this "good morning" to be for them the announcement of a good life, for your consolation and for mine, and for the consolation of the whole church!

❧120❧

The Heart of the World

"Behold our God, to whom we looked to save us!... Let us rejoice and be glad that he has saved us!" (Is 25:9). These words from the book of Isaiah... invite us to trust in the Lord....

On the mountain of victory he is preparing a festive banquet for all peoples. Tears will be wiped away from all faces and death will be eliminated for ever. Peace will reign. Christ, Son of the Virgin Mary, will be the heart of the world.

Let us pray that the Father's will may be done, making all people children of God through the unifying action of the Spirit.

NOTES

1. *De Cain et Abel,* II 10, 38 *CSEL,* 32, 408.
2. *LG,* n. 9.
3. *LG,* n. 9.
4. *LG,* n. 9.
5. Paul VI, Discourse to the "Equipes de Notre Dame" Movement (May 4, 1970), n. 7: *AAS* 62 (1970), 432.
6. On the Family (*Familiaris Consortio;* November 22, 1981), 17; *AAS* 74 (1982), 100.
7. On the Family, 49.
8. *Confessions,* I, 1.
9. *LG,* n. 63.
10. Paul VI, Discourse (March 19, 1969): *Insegnamenti,* VII (1969), 1267.
11. See *Summa Theol.,* I-II, q. 69, a. 2.
12. *Retraite,* n. 71.
13. *Retraite,* n. 135.
14. *SC,* n. 122 and n. 123.
15. *In Johannis Evangelium Tractatus,* 21, 8: *CCL* 36, 216.
16. Paul VI, Apostolic Letter *(Alma Parens): AAS* 58 (1966), 614.
17. *Lectiones Duae 'Poenitemini,'* cited in *Alma Parens*: *AAS* 58 (1966), 614.

18. Address at Drogheda, Ireland (September 29, 1979), n. 5: *AAS* 71 (1979), II, 1079.

19. *In Matthaeum, Hom.* L, 3: *PG* 58, 508.

20. *FF,* 121.

21. *FF,* 359.

22. St. Ambrose, *Exameron,* V &, 19; CSEL 32, I, 154.

23. Paul VI, *Humanae Vitae,* 9: AAS 60 (1968), 486.

24. Sequence for Pentecost.

25. Homily for the celebration of the Eucharist in Krakow, June 10, 1979: AAS 71 (1979), 873.

26. Paul VI, Apostolic Exhortation *Evangelii Nuntiandi* (December 8, 1975), 53; AAS 68 (1976), 42.

27. Paul VI, Discourse to the Committee for the International Year of the Woman (April 18, 1975): AAS 67 (1975), 266.

28. *The Story of a Soul,* manuscript A, f. 4v.

29. Mission of the Redeemer, n. 11.

30. *De Vita Moysis,* II, 2-3: *PG* 44, 327-328.

31. Mother of the Redeemer, n. 2.

32. Paul VI, *Pensiero all Morte,* Instituto Paulo VI (Brescia, 1988), 24.

SOURCES

All selections have been taken from the official Vatican translation of papal documents. Some are from encyclicals and apostolic letters published in the United States by Pauline Books & Media. Some texts appeared originally in *L'Osservatore Romano* (English edition), which is the official Vatican newspaper, and were reprinted in *The Pope Speaks (TPS)*, a bimonthly periodical published by *Our Sunday Visitor*.

Frontispiece, Message for the Annual World Day of Prayer for Vocations (*I discepoli;* November 1, 1991), in *TPS* (Vol. 37, no. 3; May/June, 1992), 131.

1. Homily of His Holiness at the Beginning of His Ministry as Supreme Shepherd of the Church, [October 22, 1978): *AAS* 70 (1978)], 947.

2. Message in preparation for the Eighth World Youth Day (*Dopo gli incontri;* August 15, 1992) *TPS* (Vol. 38, No. 1, January/February, 1993), 40-41.

3. Message in preparation for the Eighth World Youth Day, 41.

4. *Lift Up Your Hearts* (Servant Publications, 1995), 134.

5. The Splendor of Truth (*Veritatis Splendor;* October 5, 1993), n. 15.

6. The Gospel of Life (*Evangelium Vitae;* March 25, 1995), n. 9.

7. Negotiation: The Only Realistic Solution to the Continuing Threat of War, n. 13.

8. Message to the World's Leaders and All People of Good Will (*Quale persona*), December 8, 1992, *TPS* (Vol. 38, No. 3; May June 1993), 160.

9. Mother of the Redeemer (*Redemptoris Mater;* March 25, 1987), n. 25.

10. Reconciliation and Penance (*Reconciliatio et Paenitentia;* 1992), n. 6.

11. Reconciliation and Penance, n. 10.

12. Guardian of the Redeemer (*Redemptoris Custos);* 1993), n. 7.

13. The Redeemer of Man (*Redemptor Hominis*), n. 10.

14. *Lift Up Your Hearts,* 228.

15. General Audience (*Signore*), September 9, 1992, *TPS* (Vol. 38, No.1, January/February, 1993), 44-45.

16. The Holy Spirit in the Life of the Church and the World (*Dominum et Vivificantem*), n. 65.

17. The Splendor of Truth, n. 107.

18. "Behold, your Mother," Letter to Priests (Holy Thursday 1988), n. 4.

19. Guardian of the Redeemer, n. 25-26.

20. The Lay Members of Christ's Faithful People (*Christifideles Laici*), n. 58.

21. Address on the mystery of the Church *(La realta),* No. 90 in *TPS* (Vol. 39, No. 5; September/October 1994), 317.

22. *Lift Up Your Hearts,* 153.

23. Homily on the Canonization of Blessed Claude La Colombiere *(Cristo Prega),* May 31, 1992 in *TPS* (Vol. 38, No. 1; January/February, 1993), 15-16.

24. *Lift Up Your Hearts,* 49.

25. *Lift Up Your Hearts,* 46-47.

26. On the Dignity & Vocation of Women *(Mulieris Dignitatem),* n. 16.

27. Mother of the Redeemer, n. 46.

28. *Lift Up Your Hearts,* 233-234.

29. The Splendor of Truth, n. 21.

30. On the Family *(Familiaris Consortio),* n. 86.

31. *Sunday Angelus* (December 4, 1994), *L'Osservatore Romano* (English edition: December. 7, 1994), 1.

32. The Splendor of Truth, n. 118.

33. *Lift Up Your Hearts,* 59.

34. Reconciliation and Penance, n. 4.

35. Homily During the Beatification Ceremonies of John Duns Scotus (March 21, 1993) in *TPS* (Vol. 38, No. 4; (July/August, 1993), 246-47.

36. On Human Work *(Laborem Exercens),* n. 25.

37. On Human Work, n. 27.

38. General Audience (September 7, 1994) in *TPS* (Vol. 40, No. 1; January-February 1995), 37-38.

39. The Gospel of Life, n. 94.

40. The Splendor of Truth, n. 22, 23.

41. Negotiation, n. 11.

42. On Social Concern *(Solicitudo Rei Socialis),* n. 24.

43. Message for the 1992 World Day of Youth (November 30, 1991) in *TPS* (Vol. 37, No.3; May/June, 1995), 139.

44. Message for 1992 World Day of Youth, 141.

45. The Gospel of Life, n. 87.

46. The Splendor of Truth n. 9, 11.

47. Mission of the Redeemer, 46.

48. The Holy Spirit in the Life of the Church and the World, n. 55.

49. *Lift Up Your Hearts,* 245.

50. Mother of the Redeemer, n. 23 and n. 45.

51. The Gospel of Life, n. 41.

52. The Gospel of Life, n. 99.

53. *Lift Up Your Hearts,* 102.

54. On the Family, n. 25.

55. On the Family, n. 44.

56. Catechesis in Our Time, 72.

57. On Human Work, 52-53.

58. The Mercy of God, n. 7.

59. The Mercy of God, n. 14.

60. The Splendor of Truth, n. 18.

61. *Lift Up Your Hearts,* 100.

62. Reconciliation and Penance, n. 31.

63. *Lift Up Your Hearts,* 50.

64. *Lift Up Your Hearts,* 115.

65. Address on mystery of the Church, No.91 (*Nella precedente;* June 15, 1994) in *TPS* (Vol. 39, No. 6; November/December, 1994), 378.

66. The Redeemer of Man, n. 18.

67. Reconciliation and Penance, n. 9.

68. Mission of the Redeemer, n. 7 & n. 8.

69. Letter to Families for the 1994 Year of the Family in *TPS* (Vol. 39, No. 4; July/August, 1994), 234.

70. Address to the Ninth International Conference organized by the Pontifical Council for Pastoral Assistance to Health-Care Workers (Nov. 26, 1994) in *L'Osservatore Romano* (English edition: December 7, 1994), 4.

71. The Mercy of God, n. 2.

72. The Mercy of God, n. 3.

73. Mission of the Redeemer, 14.

74. *Lift Up Your Hearts,* 43.

75. The Lay Members of Christ's Faithful People, 49.

76. Address on the Mystery of the Church, No.94 (*Tutti i seguaci;* July 13, 1994) in *TPS* (Vol. 39, No. 6; November/December, 1994), 386.

77. *Message to the World's Leaders and All People of Good Will,* 160.

78. A letter to the Poor Clares (August 11, 1993) in *TPS,* (Vol. 39, No. 2; March/April, 1994), 73-74, 76.

79. On the Dignity and Vocation of Women *(Mulieris Dignitatem),* n. 21.

80. I Will Give You Shepherds *(Pastores Dabo Vobis),* n. 8.

81. Address to the Religious Alliance Against Pornography (January 30, 1992) in *TPS* (Vol. 37, No. 4; July/August, 1992), 207-8.

82. Sunday Angelus Message, *L'Osservatore Romano* (English edition: December 7, 1994), 1.

83. Message for 1994 World Mission Day (May 22, 1994) in *TPS* (Vol. 39, No. 6; November/December, 1994) 364-65.

84. General Audience (January 25, 1995), *L'Osservatore Romano* (English edition: February 1, 1995), 11.

85. *Lift Up Your Hearts,* 239-240.

86. The Mystery and Worship of the Eucharist *(Dominicae Cenae),* n. 5.

87. Homily at Mass for International Youth Forum (August 14, 1993) in *TPS* (Vol. 39, No. 1; January/February, 1994), 4-5.

88. Address to an International Congress on Care of the Dying (March 17, 1992) in *TPS* (Vol. 37, No. 4; July /August, 1992), 243.

89. Address to Members of the Diplomatic Corps (January 15, 1994), in *TPS* (Vol. 39, No. 3; (May/June, 1994), 191.

90. The Lay Members of Christ's Faithful People, n. 41.

91. Mission of the Redeemer, n. 51.

92. The Gospel of Life, n. 70

93. I Will Give You Shepherds, n. 19.

94. *Lift Up Your Hearts,* 227.

95. Reconciliation and Penance, n. 15.

96. Reconciliation and Penance, n. 16.

97. *Lift Up Your Hearts,* 158-59.

98. The Splendor of Truth, n. 71.

99. On the Family, n. 11.

100. The Gospel of Life, n. 92.

101. Arrival speech to the President of the United States on the Eighth World Youth Day (August 12, 1993) in *TPS* (Vol. 39, No. 2; March/April, 1994), 85-86.

102. General Audience on the mystery of the Church, no. 97 (August 3, 1994), in *TPS* (Vol. 40, No.1; January/February, 1995), 28-29.

103. Letter for the 1994 Year of the Family (February 2, 1994) in *TPS* (Vol. 39, No. 4; July/August, 1994), 216.

104. *Lift Up Your Hearts,* 54.

105. The Gospel of Life, n. 38.

106. Message for World Communications Day (January 24, 1994) in *TPS* (Vol. 39, No. 4; July/August, 1994), 205.

107. Mission of the Redeemer, n. 92.

108. Message for the Third World Day of the Sick (November 21, 1994) in *L'Osservatore Romano* (English edition: December 7, 1994), 3.

109. On Social Concern, n. 40.
110. Mission of the Redeemer, 11.
111. The Gospel of Life, n. 84.
112. *Lift Up Your Hearts,* 310.
113. The Redeemer of Man, 11.
114. *Lift Up Your Hearts,* 153-54.
115. The Gospel of Life *(Evangelium Vitae:* March 25, 1995), n. 51.
116. Mission of the Redeemer, 86.
117. The Holy Spirit in the Life of the Church and the World, n. 67.
118. *Lift Up Your Hearts,* 112.
119. *Lift Up Your Hearts,* 135-36.
120. Homily for the closing of the Week of Prayer for Christian Unity (January 25, 1992) in *TPS* (Vol. 37, No. 3; May/June, 1992), 184-85.